Grasp:

Making Sense of Science and Spirituality

Jim Trainor

Grasp

*Making Sense
of Science and Spirituality*

Jim Trainor

By Jim Trainor

Grasp: Making Sense of Science and Spirituality (2010)

Waverly's Universe (2012)

The Sand People (2013)

Up North (2014)

The Mountain Goat (2017)

68: A Novel (2018)

More information on these books may be found at
www.JimTrainorAuthor.com

For Mary

Grasp: Making Sense of Science and Spirituality

Author's Note: In order to protect the privacy of friends and colleagues, certain details used in personal stories – names, professions, chronology, etc. – have been changed.

ISBN 978-1-456-35408-4

Grasp:
Making Sense of Science and Spirituality

Contents

Preface

You are a student of life. You have big questions: Why are we here? How did we get here? What is the nature, the origin, the purpose of this vast mysterious 'here' we call the universe? Each of these questions is important, and they underlie all the lesser daily questions with which we each struggle. Some of you may look to science for the answers to these big questions. Others may look to historical evidence. Some of you may seek spiritual answers. Some of you may look to both the scientific and spiritual realm. Some of you may be uncertain where to look. But we are all observing, and we all have questions.

I worked as a professional physicist for nearly thirty years. I sought my answers in the purity of the laws and scientific processes of physics, which seeks to identify the relationships between matter and energy that underpin all the other natural sciences (chemistry, biology, geology and so on). I was privileged to serve with some of the brightest scientists in some of the premier research institutions in the world. I had the opportunity to work on cutting-edge research programs, to test physics theories with state-of the art experiments, to argue through ideas at international conferences and publish findings in the best science journals. I have pulled my share of all-nighters collecting data in the lab. I know the frustration of an experiment that fails after all your hard work, and I have occasionally experienced the euphoria of an experiment that succeeded, shining new light onto our understanding of physical reality. Working as a physicist is tough, exciting and utterly a blast!

So maybe you can imagine the raised eyebrows I encountered when I told my colleagues, friends and family that I would leave experimental physics research to study theology and become the pastor of a church. "How could you possibly do that? Those two things sure don't seem related to each other!" Underlying such comments, I suspect, has often been a deeper question: "How could someone grounded in modern scientific principles and practices possibly become fascinated with something so ancient, so mysterious, so soft and unprovable as religion?" As if modern science and spirituality are somehow in such conflict that you must choose one or the other.

This book is my answer to that question. And I will tell you at the outset that science and religion are not in conflict, but rather take different paths which both seek the truth. There is a popular notion that rational scientific inquiry is slowly and relentlessly eroding away what has been seen as ancient spiritual truths. From my perspective this popular notion holds no water.

Grasp is written for everyone who has pondered the big questions mentioned above, for everyone who has questioned whether science and spirituality are antagonists or partners in unveiling the mysteries of our existence. *Grasp* attempts to provide the reader space to explore and question through a fresh prism. The discussions engaged here are for those from any, or no, faith tradition, and they assume no background in either science or theology. For people of faith, this work should bring encouragement to those with lurking concerns that somehow modern scientific discoveries suggest that their ancient religious faith is obsolete. For the agnostic or atheist, this book attempts to open avenues of objective inquiry into mystery beyond what can be grasped through scientific investigation alone. Many people fall in between. While not professing a specific religious belief, they are interested in exploring the spiritual life, seeking after spiritual truth. For them, I hope this book will prompt questioning that draws them deeper into their quest. For everyone, the book collects the thoughts of great thinkers, both religious and scientific—believers, unbelievers, and those in between—all who have wrestled with these issues.

Somehow we've gotten to the place where there is a perceived conflict between science and spirituality. How did we get to this place? Is such a conflict real or is it an illusion? In order to understand all this, it will be necessary to review the ways we come to know the truth about anything, whether it is scientific or spiritual. This will be done in Chapters 1-3. Then we will also need to examine a bit of history to see how the tension between science and faith has developed. We'll take this up in Chapter 4.

From there we will dive in to explore the reality of our universe, seeking to grasp the truth. To understand the impact of modern physics on religious faith, we will look at some of the amazing discoveries in physics over the past one hundred years. What's been learned has revolutionized the way we must look at reality. Surprisingly, we will see that despite a great explosion in understanding, in some ways we have less confidence in our scientific understanding of reality today than we did a hundred years ago. At the beginning of the twentieth century our culture was very confident about the understanding of physical reality that science had developed. The great Russian physicist Lev Landau once quipped that physicists are "often wrong but never uncertain." We will see that a lot of that "certainty" has been lost—and replaced by wonder and awe—as we have begun to learn how incredibly complex reality is. I believe this complexity may be at least a hint of the glory of God.

Einstein once said that a theory should be as simple as possible, but no simpler. I've attempted to follow that guidance here. For the reader who wants to go deeper, many references are provided, and I've included a brief list of readable books I've found especially helpful in understanding these fields and their relationship.

I have spent considerable time serving hands-on in two amazing worlds: the world of physics research and in the church as a pastor. And so I write not so much to provide a comprehensive text book on either science or theology (there are many good resources for that), but to provide a perspective on both and how they relate to each other—and how one can delight in both—in our modern complex world. My perspective comes from my religious tradition as a Christian, but the ideas presented here apply equally well to any faith in a sovereign creator God.

In this book I share stories about professional physicists and their search for meaning in life and their encounters with God. As these are very personal stories, I use fictitious names and places to conceal the identities of these people. In all cases I have the most profound admiration for my brothers and sisters who serve in the very challenging and important field of physics. I also share the stories of great physicists who deeply affected our history and the very way we think about reality. Interwoven with these stories are my story, your story, and the story of God.

1. Knowledge and Faith

Last night I sat on a small dock on a Northern Wisconsin lake, looking in awe at the stars. It was a moonless night, far from the light of any town. The sky was alive with stars! As a physicist, I am even more astounded by the scene, knowing that all the stars I can see (maybe ten thousand?) are only a tiny fraction of the stars (a hundred million?) in one galaxy, our own Milky Way. And that this, my home galaxy, is only one rather typical galaxy among the million times a million galaxies in the known universe. This knowledge could make me feel inconsequential, but that's not the case on this night. Instead, the scene makes me feel like a part—and not a negligible part, but an essential part—of the great cosmos.

I silently said a prayer, thanking God for allowing me to be a part of all this. I was confident that my prayer had been heard. But why such confidence? Out beyond, or within, all those stars, or very nearby, or in another dimension: is there a God who is responsible for all that I see and hear on this spectacular night? A God who is responsible for the stars, but also the melancholy cry of a loon, the soft June breeze rustling the towering white pines behind me, the peaceful sleep of my son in the nearby cabin, and the gentle lapping of the water against the dock? This question is of utmost importance to me, and perhaps to you as well, because I also want to know that this very same God, who created the cosmos and created me, cares about me and holds me—tiny me in the midst of a billion trillion burning suns—in the palm of his hand. Can a physicist like me have any justification for believing (or hoping for) such things? Can an intelligent reader like you believe such things with confidence, in light of what science has taught us about reality in this incredible universe?

Some would say yes, that a well-informed 21st century person can have a faith in a living God. Some would say no. Richard Feynman, one of the great physicists of the twentieth century, said no. Feynman, an outspoken and original thinker and a major contributor to our understanding of physical reality, said there is an inherent conflict between science and religion. Here's how he saw this conflict developing in a person's life.[1] A young person, raised in a family of religious belief, goes to college, where he or she studies science. There she encounters two factors which challenge her faith. First, she learns how to think critically and to doubt, leading to doubts about her own faith. Secondly, the student acquires knowledge about the universe (its size and properties and so on), which seems to make the idea of a creator God less necessary. Yes, it began that way for me too.

But that's not the way it ended up. Just like the young person Feynman talked about, I was raised in a family that taught me about God. Later, I too went to the university, where I learned to question and analyze and think like a scientist. I learned to question what I had been taught as a child, and I did. I learned to think for myself, and I learned to benefit from great scholars in many disciplines. I went through a period of rethinking and even rebelling against much of what I had always taken for granted. Yes, I learned about the infinite complexity of the universe, but this is where Feynman and I seem to part ways. I never came to the same crisis of faith, as the young person Feynman described, for I had developed a relationship with God. Oh, I had learned about God's love from my parents, but as I proceeded in my studies, I went on a spiritual journey as well. In this journey, through times of personal trial and even depression, this remote God of my parents and the Church became a real God who meets me wherever I am and loves me through it.

This didn't happen overnight or even by a progression of clear steps. It came from many prayers, which sometimes seemed to go unanswered. It came from learning about Scripture, even through the many times when I didn't look at a Bible for months. It came from seeing God's love in the faces of other people, even though many times I was so preoccupied with my own problems that I could not recognize it. But somehow, in spite of my spiritual laziness and tendency to wander off the path, I developed faith—both a *knowing* of God's reality and a *trust* in God's active presence in my life. I no more needed to verify whether God existed than to verify that my own mother existed. On that dock in northern Wisconsin, there was no doubt at all that this same God who put those stars and galaxies in the sky, had also heard my prayer.

Yet, my response to Feynman's position may come across as a bit too glib and neatly wrapped-up for your tastes. That's okay. Feynman raised a critical question that we cannot ignore. It is a question that I could not ignore, and in fact it lies at the heart of understanding the intersection of science and faith. How, in fact, do we know if something is true? How do we know if a hypothesis in physics is valid or not? How do we know if faith is built upon truth or not?

Perhaps there is one set of truths that apply to science and another set that apply to the spiritual life? No, truth is truth. There cannot be one truth that pertains to science and another truth that pertains to faith. The truth of one will not contradict the other. Stephen Jay Gould, historian and biologist, speaks of science and religion both pursuing truth as part of "our shared struggle for wisdom in all its various guises."[2] This does not mean that science and faith can be used interchangeably to understand reality. A religious faith tradition can no more be used to confirm the predictions of quantum mechanics than can quantum mechanics be used to instruct me how I should treat my neighbor. Yet, science and faith do not exclude one another either, but in fact, as we shall see, may enable each other. Believers in God should not bury their heads in the sand and pretend that scientific discoveries do not exist. And nonbelievers should not be too hasty in waving off ideas beyond what can be proved in the laboratory or verified mathematically (the domains of science), dismissing them into a lesser realm of philosophy or religion—this can be a sort of tunnel vision that limits our grasp of truth. Truth is truth.

I began to explore the question of whether the advances in modern science still allow a traditional faith in God only after many years. I was trained as a physicist and worked much of my adult life as a professional physicist, and even though I have also been a Christian since childhood, for a long time I kept those two sides of my life fairly separate. I was caught up in the busy life of physics research during the day, and then I would have my religious faith on the side. It was like I had a sort of split personality, and I never gave a thought about the need to connect my passion for science with my faith in God. In fact, it was only after I became an ordained pastor that I began to seriously recognize that I needed to better understand the relationship between the worlds of science and religious faith.

So, a huge question is on the table: in light of all of the discoveries of science over the past century, can anyone believe in a God understood in our religious faith traditions or revealed in Scripture, a collection of ancient books thousands of years old? Is the biblical understanding of life and of God a relic of ancient history and primitive thinking that has now been made obsolete? In my Christian tradition, the Bible is described as "the revealed word of God." 3 In light of modern physics, can anyone believe this is true? More generally, how do we know that anything is true? The answer to this question lies at the heart of understanding the relationship between science and faith. We will take this up in the next two chapters. But before we discuss *how* we know, let's talk about *what* we know (and what we don't know).

Whad'Ya Know? The Realms of Knowledge

Let's imagine that we can write down all possible knowledge on a single page (both things that are known and unknown to us), as in Figure 1 below. Now let's draw a circle around all of what is presently known. Within this small circle would be the altitude of Mt. Everest and the fact that it's the highest mountain in the world, how to prepare a vaccine for smallpox, and the number of games won by the Green Bay Packers in 2009. This region of knowledge is continually increasing, as indicated by the arrows pointing outward. This region of present knowledge is expanding out into a second region of things that we know that we don't know, but are seeking answers to, such as the cure for cancer or experimental verification of the latest physics theory. There's a long list of things for which humankind is seeking answers, and you and I also have a long personal list as well: How do I plan for my retirement? How do I get rid of the weeds in my back yard? How do I tell my boss I need a raise? How do I find love and meaning in my life?

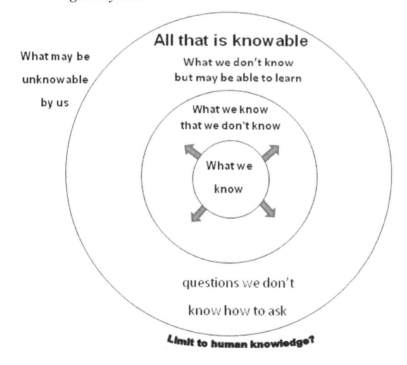

Figure 1 – Realms of knowledge.

Beyond the second circle, which encompasses the knowledge that we are seeking, is a regime of all things that could be known—of all things that are knowable—but that we don't even know how to ask about yet. Fifty years ago, for example, we didn't know how to ask a question about the internet, because it didn't exist and we couldn't imagine that it ever would exist, and yet that was knowledge that would someday be within human grasp. So there is a third regime of knowledge (that hopefully someday we're going to have), all of the answers to questions we don't even know how to ask yet.

One question this third region of knowledge space raises is: Is there a limit to human knowledge? Is there a boundary beyond which we cannot go because our ability to learn has a limit? Is there such a limit? Or, are we smart enough, or are we educable enough, that we can keep learning forever? While we do not know the answer to this question, I want to tell you about my dog, Barnabas, a beautiful Golden Retriever. I think Barnabas is surely the smartest Golden Retriever in the whole world. Maybe I'm a little biased, but I do believe he is one very bright canine! Yet, despite my attempts over and over again, Barnabas has never been able to grasp trigonometry. There is just no way he can do it. Now, what I want to ask you is why would Barnabas, who's a pretty smart dog (in fact, sometimes I think he's smarter than I am), have a limit to what he can grasp? I wonder if on some future day we may get to the point where our brainpower just can't deal with any further knowledge, even with all the benefits of advanced education, computer simulations, and whatever else may come along. The Bible claims, "The secret things belong to the Lord our God, but the revealed things belong to us and to our children forever."[4] Perhaps there are some things that you and I aren't ever going to be able to know intellectually, no matter how smart we are, no matter how much research money we invest, no matter how big our computers. No matter what, perhaps some things may always be beyond our grasp.

A Realm of Higher Ways?

So there may be another region on our page of all knowledge that includes things that are unknowable by us. In this realm may be phenomena like miracles. Perhaps actions like God's intervention into our world. If this is true, people who believe in God must be careful to avoid the mistake of attempting to explain what may be termed miracles (such as apparent healings after prayer) and other 'secret things' (perhaps such as the working of the Holy Spirit and the nature of the soul). For example, when physicists speak of the extra dimensions that are predicted by string theory, some clever theologian may say, "Aha! See, God can work through those extra dimensions! That's how God can be everywhere at once!" When we make an argument like that, we're limiting God to the small domain of what we humans already know, the small inner circle in Figure 1. Now, do the extra dimensions predicted by string theory provide God with access across the universe? I have no idea, and probably I never will, but God can do whatever God wants. While it may be amusing to speculate how God acts, let's be careful not to build arguments for God's existence and actions upon our present finite realm of knowledge. Scientific understanding is continually maturing, so don't run the real risk of basing a case for God upon an argument that may soon be weak or obsolete.

St. Thomas Aquinas, a thirteenth-century theologian, was an eloquent champion in developing arguments for the existence and nature of God. Yet he cautioned that "bad arguments for God's existence do more harm than good, since they give unbelievers an occasion to laugh." Aquinas said we lose ground when we argue for a truth based on something that may be later proved untrue because "the very inadequacy of the arguments would rather strengthen them in error, since they would imagine that our acceptance of the truth of faith was based on such weak arguments." [5]

The prophet Isaiah presents these words from God: *"As the heavens are higher than the earth, are my ways higher than your ways, and my thoughts than your thoughts."* [6] The way God operates may be real and reliable, but on a level that we may never be able to grasp intellectually! Maybe that troubles our inquiring minds, but I don't think it should at all. I actually do know how to do trigonometry, but Barnabas doesn't and probably never will. Yet, that does not limit him in having a loving and full relationship with me. Even though Barnabas doesn't know the difference between a tangent and a tangerine, in some ways he knows me, as man's best friend, better than many people do. God seeks the deepest of relationships with us. "Come to me" (e.g., Matthew 11:28) is the pervasive invitation from God. And God gives us ways to respond, to enter into the deepest of realities, a place that God promises is filled with rest, power, joy, healing, and love. Though our brains, and computers, and particle accelerators may be too small to ever unravel the way God works—to truly know the mind of God (as one famous astrophysicist hopes for)[7] —yet we are invited into the higher ways of God. While I am fascinated by the world of physics and I inquire and study and cheer the great work ongoing, even more I want to know God and his mysterious higher ways, ways that include a plan for my life and a destiny for me and all of creation.

It is not unintellectual to acknowledge mystery. Just because something is a mystery (that is, we cannot explain all the details), doesn't mean it isn't true—this holds for theology and it holds for physics. A good example is the understanding of a property of some solids called superconductivity. Below a certain temperature some metals exhibit the amazing property of suddenly losing all their resistance to electric current. That is, if you cool certain metals—such as aluminum—to very low temperatures, you will reach a certain temperature where the metal has a finite resistance to electrical current passing through it, but then if the temperature is reduced even a tiny fraction lower (say a thousandth of a degree), suddenly all the electrical resistance vanishes. The metal has become a perfect conductor of electricity, a superconductor. While the phenomenon of superconductivity occurs in many metals, in many other metals (such as silver or copper) it does not. This is more than just an intellectual curiosity, it has great potential practical importance. If power transmission lines could be made out of superconducting material (and we're still a ways off from that becoming a reality), then the efficiency of power transmission across the country could be increased perhaps tenfold.

This strange phenomenon of superconductivity was discovered nearly a hundred years ago, but for nearly fifty years after its discovery no one could come up with an acceptable explanation of just what causes superconductivity to occur. Superconductivity exists, everyone agreed, but no one could explain it. It was a mystery. In the 1950s an elegant explanation of superconductivity was finally published[8]--based upon a novel new understanding of how electrons in metals interact with each other through the vibrating metal ions in a solid. The mystery of superconductivity – at least for some materials – had been solved and led to a richly deserved Nobel Prize in Physics. Scientists at last began to feel they really understood the mystery of superconductivity, even though its reality had not been in doubt from the beginning.

Believers in God realize that mystery is a part of faith. Scripture says that "the mystery of our religion is great,"[9] and that our perception of God is as if we're looking in "a mirror dimly."[10] Physicists continually confront mystery, without sacrifice of intellectual dignity. When those who believe in a sovereign God acknowledge the mystery of faith, they in no way are conceding the reality of the foundations upon which that faith is built. Just because you cannot explain a certain Bible passage, or understand what happens in a sacrament, or produce a theory that lays out how prayer works, doesn't mean that your faith is not grounded upon reality. Albert Einstein describes beautifully the power of mystery:

> The most beautiful emotion we can experience is the mysterious. It is the most fundamental emotion that stands at the cradle of all true art and science. He to whom this emotion is a stranger, who can no longer wonder and stand rapt in awe, is as good as dead, a snuffed-out candle. [11]

Mystery—awe and recognition of that which we cannot explain, yet hold to be true—stands at the center of both faith and science. The wordless beauty of a cathedral, the "sublime, subtle and inexplicable" that Einstein saw behind the laws of physics,[12] the twinkle in a baby's eye, the astounding reality that in the midst of a vast and complex universe, you and I are here.

2. How Do I Know What's True?

If both science and spirituality seek the truth, then it's necessary for us to ask, How do we know what is true and what is untrue? How do we know whether a new scientific conjecture is true or untrue? How do we know if the claims of religious faith are true or untrue? As we examine the ways of knowing, we will see, as surprising as it may seem, that there is some commonality between the ways of knowing scientific truth and knowing truth about God.

There are at least three objective processes commonly used to determine truth, ways to find concrete answers to concrete questions. There is a fourth process to determine truth, a more subjective method that is relational, personal, intuitive and holistic – and it may apply to the deepest questions we have. But let's first look at the objective methods, all guided by the scientific method, which is the foundation of modern objective investigation. With the scientific method we experimentally test hypotheses, our best informed conjecture about the truth. For example, we might test the hypothesis that "it is raining outside" with the experiment of simply going outside and setting up a rain gauge or just looking out the window to observe directly if it's raining. Or we might observe the possible effects of our hypothesis. ("I conclude that it's raining outside, because Sally just came inside and she is soaked!") A third process for determining truth is listening to credible witnesses ("I know it's raining outside, because David just told me and I believe him.").

Of course, all three of these methods must be used carefully: we might conclude that it is not raining because we set up the rain gauge underneath a tree (a bad experiment), or we may conclude that it is raining because Sally walked through the sprinkler (drawing the wrong conclusion from looking at the effects) or because David didn't tell us the truth (the witness was not credible). Establishing the truth often requires repeated experiments, confirmation by alternate means, and questioning of our methods – and certainly being careful how we treat hearsay, speculation passed off as fact, or claims that may be dishonest.

The First Process: Direct Observation

A famous example of test by direct observation is Galileo's study of the laws of falling bodies. He was only a first year student at the University of Pisa (probably around 1589, when he was about 24) when he hypothesized that the way falling objects are accelerated by gravity does not depend on their mass, contrary to the common sense of many people of his day.[1] He was not content to rest his ideas upon speculation, however, and decided to do an experiment by dropping objects of different sizes and weights from the Leaning Tower of Pisa, while someone at the bottom determined whether the objects arrived at the ground simultaneously. The experiment indeed confirmed Galileo's hypothesis. However, what if Galileo's experiment had consisted of dropping a cannon ball and a feather? In this case, there would have been additional effects (for example, how the motion of the feather is affected by air currents or the buoyancy of the air) that would have prevented a conclusive test. This would have been a bad experiment. Galileo was too smart to make this mistake.

You might correctly say that Galileo's experiment only proved that the acceleration of gravity was proved to be the same for the specific objects he used; maybe for other-sized objects gravity behaves differently. That would be an additional hypothesis you could test, but of course you could carry this on ad infinitum. Galileo's belief about gravity was only made solid and universal when Isaac Newton mathematically described the force of gravity for all bodies a hundred years later. Of course, more modern experiments and theories would show that Newton's understanding would have to be modified, leading to yet newer theories. Such is the beautiful interplay between experiment and theory and the means by which scientific knowledge advances.

One well-known practitioner of the scientific method approach to determining truth was Lieutenant Columbo. Remember the disheveled, cigar-smoking TV detective Columbo? He was a guy who could find a little clue that others had missed - the single strand of hair lying on the sofa, or the little smudge on the window, and by forensic study of tiny shreds of evidence he would discover the truth. Beginning with the evidence, sometimes quite scant, Columbo would form a hypothesis (often not revealed to the viewer until the last five minutes of the show): perhaps the single strand of hair came from the killer. The hypothesis was tested with experiments, which, for Lt. Columbo, were performed in the crime lab. He was always sending evidence off to the crime lab, and at a key moment in the show, he'd get a call that verified that the muddy left shoe did indeed belong to the suspect.

In physics we do the same kind of thing, as we seek to understand reality. Physicists began with simple views of reality, and through centuries of careful investigation (never overlooking the smudge on the window) developed better explanations of reality, right up to the present day of advanced theories about the underlying reality of the universe. And no doubt, this process will continue into the future (just as the history of science has revealed surprise upon surprise, we expect the future of science to be no different!).

There have been huge triumphs using the scientific method, but there's one limitation to this approach for determining the truth. It only works for phenomena that are reproducible, that is, that happen over and over again the same way, like dropping cannon balls off the top of the Leaning Tower of Pisa. We could go to Pisa, Italy, today and repeat Galileo's experiment and get the same result he did. But what if the laws of physics were such that the acceleration a falling body experiences was different every time? Then the scientific method might not work for this problem, would it? We parents have sometimes made a similar logical error in raising our children—at least I have made it with my three children. We are not given an instruction manual with our first child. We learn by many ways how to responsibly rear that child. As the child flourishes into a beautiful young person, we may falsely conclude that we now know how to raise children. Then the second child comes along, and she's totally different. All the knowledge we gained with the first child about sleeping habits, disposition, appetite, discipline and so on must be relearned, because each child is unique.

What if there are phenomena that occur so infrequently and are of a nature that we cannot reproduce them in the laboratory? How would you examine such things by the scientific method? For example, a rare phenomenon that occurs out on the sea is the water spout, which is an oceanic tornado in which huge amounts of water are taken into the air. There are ancient legends of ships being lifted out of the sea by water spouts—sort of like the Pecos Bill stories from the old southwest. Many of these stories reached superstitious proportions, like the ancient tales of sea monsters. For centuries it was believed that water spouts were just fantasies of imaginative sailors who'd been out to sea a little too long. But indeed, water spouts exist and have been observed many times and recorded on film in the past hundred years. They're just too rare to be observed very often and too difficult to reproduce in a laboratory experiment.

What if there are phenomena that occur only once? That is, they are not reproducible, so that we might observe them subsequently (as with water spouts) or design an experiment to test the hypothesis (like Galileo did at Pisa). Phenomena like the resurrection of Christ, which happened only once. Although there has been a great deal of scientific investigation into the life of Christ, the truth or untruth of the resurrection cannot be determined by direct observation or test through experiment.

Yet, there are objective, scientific ways that shed light on the truth of the resurrection, as we'll now see.

The Second Process: Looking at the Effects

Often a truth may not be determined by direct observation. In such cases we may design an experiment that looks at the effects that would occur if our hypothesis is true. If the expected effects are observed and if we can eliminate other explanations for these effects, we have evidence that the hypothesis is true. Such objective investigation helps us determine truth in science and faith.

For example, might we grasp the truth of the resurrection by examining its effects upon the lives of those who were there at the time it occurred? We should expect that such a startling and unexpected event would dramatically affect the lives of those people. If the resurrection of Christ did not occur, then we would expect to see little effect on the lives of those who were present at that time. The Bible tells us that eleven apostles were witnesses to the resurrection, and St. Paul states (1 Corinthians 15) that over 500 other people also observed the resurrected Christ. What happened to these followers of Jesus after the resurrection? Church historians agree that most of the apostles were killed for their faith. Perhaps only St. John lived to old age and died naturally, but suffered in exile for his faith. Somehow, this group of ordinary men (fishermen and tax collectors) became courageous enough to become martyrs. Where did such courage come from? You look at the effects, and you must conclude that something truly life-changing occurred in first-century Palestine to cause such a dramatic change in the apostles' lives. When Peter and John, simple fishermen from the rural northern region of Israel, were arrested and brought before the religious authorities, they testified boldly, unafraid of possible imprisonment and threats of violence, and the authorities were astonished: "Now when they saw the boldness of Peter and John and realized that they were uneducated and ordinary men, they were amazed and recognized them as companions of Jesus."[3] We conclude that something transforming happened to these men, perhaps something as dramatic as someone rising from the dead.

The Bible says that "we are surrounded by so great a cloud of witnesses. . .,"[4] men and women from all times in whom we can see the effects of a true gospel. People like the apostles, St. Augustine, St. Francis and Ignatius Loyola, Martin Luther and Mother Teresa, and many others in whose lives we see the effects of a gospel that is true. In response to the encouragement and affirmation we receive from seeing the effects of the gospel on these people, the writer of the Hebrews tells us, "Let us also lay aside ever weight and the sin that clings so closely and let us run with perseverance the race that is set before us, looking to Jesus." St. Francis once said, "Preach the gospel and if necessary use words." The impact of the gospel in tangible and observable ways is a dramatic indication of its truth.

Determining the truth by looking at the effects is not unique to issues of faith. It's actually a tried and true method for understanding physics, actually part of the scientific method. Let's consider the example of a tiny subatomic particle called the neutrino, which means "little neutral one." It is one of the smallest objects known in nature. The neutrino has no electrical charge and very little mass, perhaps no mass at all. In fact, no one has ever seen a neutrino. You can't pick one up or put it in a jar because they are so tiny. Neutrinos cannot be directly observed, the way even atoms might be observed through exotic microscopes or the way we might see the tracks of charged particles in nuclear physics detectors. Yet, we know for a fact that neutrinos exist. How?

Neutrinos are generated and used routinely in physics experiments around the world. Yet, the neutrino is such a tiny object that the only way that you can know a neutrino exists is by observing its effect on other particles.[5] Physicists use experiments at particle accelerators and sensitive detectors to study the interactions between larger particles that have known mass and electrical charge. By the way these particles behave, scientists can conclude – with confidence – that a neutrino was present, even though it showed up only as "a ghostly presence."[6] From the reactions of the other particles, a lot can be learned about the nature of the neutrino, even though the presence of the 'little neutral one' is only inferred from its effects.

So, just how big is a neutrino? How much does a neutrino weigh, if indeed a neutrino weighs anything at all (this is still a hotly debated question)? Let's get calibrated: A teaspoon of water weighs about five grams. Let's go down from there to the neutrino level. A grain of sand weighs about 1/100th of a gram. A microscopic bacterium weighs only about one billionth of a gram. You'd have to pile 10 million bacteria onto the scale to equal one grain of sand! Yet a bacterium weighs at least a billion times a billion times a billion times as much as a neutrino! In grams, that's less than a one with 36 zeroes in front of it![6] Even the tiny subatomic electron weighs at least as much as a million neutrinos! A neutrino is so small that it will go through two million miles of lead without being stopped. So if you want to put up your neutrino shield, good luck. And right now there are billions of neutrinos bombarding your body! But I don't think you have much to worry about – they don't hurt a bit.

How could such elusive tiny particles be of any significance to us? Maybe they're just an intellectual curiosity. Think again. The neutrino is of crucial significance in the universe. It plays a role in the generation of helium in the center of stars and so it is essential to the processes that keep the sun shining. Even though a neutrino is so tiny—if it does indeed have a mass that's no more than 36 zeroes after the decimal point—there are so many of them that perhaps half of the mass of the universe is made up of neutrinos! (Neutrinos are one conjecture among physicists for the so-called dark matter of the universe). Neutrinos are significant.

The neutrino is an example of looking at the effect of an undetectable entity on a detectable entity to prove the existence and study the behavior of the entity that cannot be directly observed. No one has ever directly seen a neutrino, but by looking at the effects we can know that neutrinos exist. No one has ever seen God, but might we know of God's existence by looking at the effects of God on the lives of others?

Here's a true story about my friend Alexander. Alexander was a sophisticated leader of research who came to learn much by seeing the effects. He'd been raised as a Christian, but he hadn't been involved in church in many years. He'd become so caught up in his scientific research and all the hard work of building his career that he never gave religion a thought any more. Alexander had a great family - a beautiful wife and lovely children. But then his teenaged son started getting into trouble. Maybe some of you have had such challenges in your families, too - it happens too often. The son began to get in trouble despite his good upbringing, because Alexander had done his best to be a good father. He started running with the wrong crowd, and his grades plummeted. More and more, he was angry and confrontational and belligerent, and Alexander couldn't talk to him anymore. This was a dangerous situation, and Alexander didn't know what to do. Alexander, with all of his education, power and prestige, felt helpless.

Then one day, while Alexander's son was hanging out across the street from the high school with his rebellious friends, a young man came up and greeted him, and after a few minutes invited him to come to a youth group meeting at a local church. And for some reason, Alexander's son said he would come. He went to that youth group meeting, then again the next week. For the first time in his life, this young man heard about God. The boy's life began to change. His grades began to improve, and the anger was washed away from him. The son told his mother and father about his new faith. Alexander decided to go to one of those youth group meetings to see firsthand what was going on. Well aware of the susceptibility of youth to cults, he wanted to be sure that this was a good thing.

Alexander went and there he heard things that he hadn't heard since he was a kid himself. But mainly what the father saw were the effects on other people of a living God, long-hidden in his own life. And he saw the powerful effect of the living God upon his own son. Alexander told me this whole story while I was sitting in his office one day a few years after that youth group meeting. Alexander was a man of great intelligence and accomplishment, a man you'd expect to have all the answers – but his life was incomplete until he heard about God.

The Bible says, "Anyone who calls upon the name of the Lord will be saved, but how can they call on him to save them unless they believe in him, and how can they believe in him if they've never heard about him, and how can they hear about him unless someone tells them?"[7] Can people see the evidence of God's existence by looking at God's effect on you?

The Third Process: Witnesses

Let's turn to another process for determining truth: hearing the reports of trustworthy witnesses. Now the use of witnesses to determine truth is not so common in scientific laboratory investigation, but it is an established objective method for determining truth in forensic investigation, right alongside the use of scientific data and physical evidence. The biggest question about witnesses, of course, is: can you believe them? A good witness must be honest, competent (able to evaluate what they have seen) and objective (unbiased and rational).

Sometimes we may be unsure about the testimony of a witness. Here's a fictitious but plausible story that illustrates the dilemma we may face. A woman is called to the bedside of her mother, who is near death. During this last visit with her daughter, the mother gives her daughter an old box that the daughter has never seen before. The box had been handed down from one generation to another through the family. Inside the box are several letters written a very long time ago. As the daughter reads these letters, she pieces together a story about her great, great, great-grandmother, who lived during the American Revolutionary War. Apparently, her great-great-great grandma was a hero at Valley Forge. There was one letter in the box from a distant relative that the daughter had never heard of. There was another letter from a friend of her great, great, great-grandmother's, and there was a third letter from a soldier whose life had been saved by this heroic woman. According to the letters, she had been a nurse during the war, and she had sacrificially given of herself to save many lives. In fact this heroic woman had worked so hard—long hours in the cold, with inadequate food or rest—that she contracted pneumonia and died.

However, the only evidence that the young woman has that her distant relative ever existed or that this amazing story might be true, is these three letters - one from an obscure relative, one from a friend of her great, great, great-grandmother, and one from a soldier whose life had apparently been saved by her. The young woman's hands trembled as she held the letters, which had been cared for and handed down all these centuries to her mother, who now passed them on to her. Are these credible witnesses, these people she has never met or even heard of before? Could their testimony be trusted? How could she know for sure?

The young woman decided to go to Valley Forge National Historical Park in Pennsylvania, where many of the battle artifacts have been preserved, and investigate. It is a beautiful and nostalgic place. As she strolled the grounds, the young woman could imagine her ancient relative being there, but there was no concrete or helpful evidence. While she was in Pennsylvania, the young woman sought out old newspaper articles from the Revolutionary War era (there were some in the museums and a few old newspaper offices), but the articles she found only talked about generals and politicians - only the important people. No mention would have been there about a nurse who died of pneumonia. The woman decided to interview a historian, and she asked him whether or not this was a believable story. The historian listened carefully, then told her that the story was unlikely to be true. He said, "You might want to dismiss these fanciful tales. They're probably exaggerations, because most people don't behave as your letters claim. It happened such a long time ago! Remember these people were often superstitious and uneducated and did not have the modern sophistication that we possess. They often came up with tall tales, which usually get embellished as they are passed along." The young woman left, discouraged.

This fictitious story presents the dilemma with witnesses. On what criteria do you believe a witness? If you were that young woman, would you believe the letters she had received? I think you probably would. I think you'd believe it because you've heard from three witnesses who had nothing to gain by fabricating this story, and you have the testimony of a trusted mother who believed these witnesses.

Believers in God have a set of letters, written by witnesses. You must decide if you can believe their testimony. Here are excerpts from a couple of them. St. Paul writes:

> "I passed on to you what was most important and what had been passed on to me. Christ died for our sins, just as the Scriptures said. He was buried, and he was raised from the dead on the third day, just as the Scriptures said. He was seen by Peter and then by the twelve. After that, he was seen by more than 500 of his followers at one time, most of whom are still alive, though some have died."[2]

This account says that there were many witnesses to the resurrection of Christ.

Here's another letter—from St. John—who obviously recognizes that we demand credibility from witnesses. He writes: "We declare to you what was from the beginning, what we have heard, what we have seen with our eyes, what we have looked at and touched with our hands, concerning the word of life."[3] John says that he was there, and others were there, too. They saw it, they heard it, they felt it. The Bible tells us how Thomas wanted to put his hands into the wounds of the resurrected Christ before he would believe that it really was Jesus. John was present on that occasion too. They touched the wounds, they saw him first hand. And then John tells us, "This life was revealed, and we have seen it and testify to it, and declare to you the eternal life that was with the Father and was revealed to us."[3] St. John recognizes the importance of credible witnesses, and he's asking us to believe him.

We have to decide how and if we can believe what the witness has reported. Just as the attorneys cross-examine witnesses in the court room to get at the truth, so must we examine the reports of witnesses. As we encounter the witnesses of Scripture, we decide their credibility several ways. First, we study the Bible to understand what it says. Does the story hang together? Are there serious contradictions? Might the witnesses have ulterior motives? We talk with others about what the Bible says, asking hard questions, sharing our concerns with each other – no less rigorously than a court room cross examination. We listen to sermons in churches, and we read what historians, scholars, saints and critics have said about the Scriptures. Perhaps we study the ancient languages in which the Bible was originally written to see if this provides additional information about the account of the witnesses. We pray for wisdom from the Holy Spirit. We may try to live according to what the Bible says and see how it works (looking at effects). These are all actions that I have taken to understand the witnesses from Scripture and to decide if I believe them. I have come to believe that the Biblical witnesses have given us the truth.

Do you know that almost all crimes are solved not by forensic study following the scientific method (finding physical evidence or performing experiments in the lab), but by finding witnesses who will tell the truth? Very seldom is a crime solved exclusively by the forensic method. Even in the old Colombo episodes, the final determination of the guilty party usually came from a confession or revelation from a witness.

We recognize the importance of eyewitnesses, do we not? In modern journalistic war coverage, we have seen how television networks have emphasized embedded reporters. The eyewitness account is crucial in forensics, news coverage, and revealing the truth of the gospel.

One more thing about witnesses. The principal qualifications for being a credible witness are not scientific or intellectual superiority but rather honesty and integrity. I remember a family camping trip to the Great Sand Dunes National Park in Colorado. It's an unusual and beautiful place, where gigantic sand dunes have blown up against the western flank of the Rocky Mountains. One Sunday morning during our camping trip, my wife Mary and I wandered over to attend a short worship service, held at the campground fire circle where rangers often gave evening talks. It was early in the morning, and as I walked past the sites of sleeping campers, I certainly was thinking that I might have been better off staying curled up in my warm sleeping bag too. Only a few other campers joined us at the service. We sat on benches carved from tree trunks and waited for the minister, who I expected to see attired in some normal clergy vestments, probably from a local church. But instead, a most unlikely young man walked up to stand before us, a cowboy. He was not a well dressed minister, but rather a person wearing the shabby and rough clothes of someone who worked outside and with his hands. He spoke with such an inarticulate country drawl that we could scarcely understand him, and he apologized for not being a polished speaker. He told us that he worked as a horseshoer in a local town. Then the man began to simply tell us about the impact God had made on his life and the life of his family. A tear rolled down the face of this rough-hewn man as he shared with us his faith in a God who is living and real. By the end of his short talk, tears were pouring down the faces of every one of us gathered in the small amphitheatre. We left the area in silence, deeply moved and encouraged, knowing that we had just heard a first-hand report from a credible witness.

3. Another Way of Knowing: Knowing through Relationship

As powerful as the objective ways of knowing are, some of our most urgent questions have little to do with factual answers. They have everything to do with relationships. Consider these two examples.

If you become seriously ill, would you rather have access to an extensive medical library, filled with medical facts, or would you rather have access to a skilled doctor you can trust to make you well, even if you don't understand all the details of medical technology?

Or imagine that you are planning a trip to Toledo. There are two ways to get to Toledo. One is to get a Mapquest printout from the internet that provides all the travel directions you need. You have in hand all the factual information you need to find your way; and you can study the whole route in advance, hoping you won't miss that crucial turn in Fort Wayne. If you do miss that crucial turn, you could be in trouble. Another way to get to Toledo is to have an experienced and trustworthy guide travel in the car with you, directing you along the way. You may not personally know the details of the route, but you can depend on your guide to direct each step, trusting that you will arrive safely and enjoying the company along the way.[1]

Relationship is indeed a way we come to find answers. So, the fourth process of knowing is a relational and personal process. It involves trusting a relationship rather than (or in addition to) having facts. This trust has two sources: reputation and relationship. Initially, you trust the doctor because of her reputation (she is an acknowledged expert in her field) or because someone recommended her to you. In time you come to trust the doctor because you have known her, seen her competence, how she is there for you when you need her, how she can be counted on to provide the right help. This kind of knowledge may not provide factual data, but provides needed answers: Will everything be okay? Will my needs be met? Will I be taken care of? The answers from this kind of knowledge, according to philosopher Esther Meek, provide *confidence* related to the interpersonal knowing, as opposed to *certainty* that comes from information only (Processes 1-3).[2]

The French philosopher Henri Bergson distinguishes "two profoundly different ways of knowing a thing. The first implies moving round the subject (processes 1-3), the second that we enter it." The second way involves "a kind of intellectual sympathy by which one places oneself within an object in order to coincide with what is unique in it and consequently inexpressible."[3]

This kind of knowledge indeed may be inexpressible -- as may be the case with describing important relationships -- and attempts to do so may come across as poetic, qualitative, perhaps even vague. It is reliable knowledge nonetheless.

Our knowledge of God may often be inexpressible by us, and so we may come up short trying to understand *how* God acts or *why* God acts. Yet, our confidence in God does not depend upon these facts but rather upon *who* God is. Often we cannot understand God's actions or apparent inactions, yet the trust continues because of who God is. Gary Deddo, a chaplain at Princeton University who works with people struggling with life problems, summarizes Oxford scholar C. S. Lewis' discussion of the problem of suffering in the world:

> "If God is a personal God, the most important question to ask about that God is the question of *who* – the question of the very character of God. . . when the questions of whether, how, or why this personal God exists or acts in certain ways are considered apart from who this God is, the questions remain relatively abstract and misleading. Because God's wisdom far surpasses our own, we cannot understand why God allows certain things to

happen. But we can know the trustworthy character of God in Jesus Christ, the answer to the *who* question."4

The '*who* question' that Lewis describes is a question of relationship. Computer dating is all the rage these days. The computer matches people by their ages, interests, temperaments and so on. If there's a good match of data, the couple may decide to meet – this is necessary, because very few people would trust a long-term relationship only to the information they had from a computer about another person. The stakes are too high to trust facts and statistics only. It is only through the meeting and the subsequent personal interactions that a meaningful relationship may develop.

Knowing through relationship is the way God has often revealed himself. In lieu of data, which may satisfy intellectual curiosity, God offers himself, which satisfies our whole being. The Bible describes conversations Jesus had with his disciples on the night before he was crucified. He told them about the events that were about to unfold, his arrest, trial and execution, then reassures them by saying, "If you know me, you will know my Father also." But the apostle Philip was not quite satisfied with Jesus' words. He says to Jesus, "Lord, show us the Father, and we will be satisfied." Jesus does not remind Philip of all the evidence and proofs about his identity, but rather reminds him of the relationship. Jesus says, "Have I been with you all this time, Philip, and you still do not know me?"5

The psalmist advises, "Taste and see that the Lord is good. Happy are those who take refuge in him." Experience him, taste him, absorb him, take refuge in him. While God may be beyond our understanding, he is not beyond our experiencing him.6 When Jesus sent the disciples into the world he didn't send them with a roadmap, he sent them with himself. He told them, "I am with you always."7

Psychiatrist Karl Stern reminds us that the best approach to knowledge is to employ both the objective (informational) means and the subjective (relational) means. "The best attitude is ... to refrain from a judgment of value, and to watch out when to use which."[8]

Yes, we must use our intellect to check the relational ways of knowing, and vice versa. Our brain is important in our relationships, and many of us can think of times when using our brain a bit more might have saved us from trouble in a relationship. Are we not asked to love God with all our *heart* and our *mind*? [9] When St. Paul visited the city of Beroea, in modern-day Greece, he found them welcoming and interested in hearing his message, yet they were not ready to swallow everything they heard without thoughtful examination: "... they welcomed the message very eagerly and examined the scriptures every day to see whether these things were so."[10]

Yet, an essential part of good analysis is the intuitive, the 'gut reaction,' the hunch. What is it after all that guides formation of the hypothesis in the scientific method? Scientists are often encouraged to "think out of the box" – don't be restricted by convention, conformity, and logical deduction. But where does "out-of-the-box" thinking come from? I remember talking with one physics graduate student who had studied with the great physicist Neville Mott, one of the world's experts on how electrons behave inside metals. She told me that Mott not only had great scientific skills, but he also had developed a great intuition that came from living with the problems. The student said, "Mott seems to know what an electron is thinking." Such intuition is hard to explain, but I suspect that Professor Mott could 'know what an electron is thinking', not because of some mystical powers, but based on years of experience with the related fields of physics that gave him a good sense of what is plausible and what isn't. Such abilities are what separate the great physicists from the mere practitioners of physics.

I suspect this student's scientific development was just as influenced by studying with Professor Mott (that is, the relationship) as it was by the learning from many text books. This is why mentors are so important in science, as they are in many other fields. I was fortunate to have several fine mentors in physics, persons who didn't just hand me a book and say, "Read this," but who allowed me to work beside them, watching how they wrestled with problems, how they entered into the relationship with the subject just as Mott did with his electrons. Working beside good mentors allows the student to pick up the intangibles and the nuances that separate a real physicist from a manipulator of equations. Only through a trusted relationship could this happen.

One of the hottest research topics in modern physics today is string theory (which we'll talk more about in Chapter 9). String theory offers a promise of adding significantly to our understanding of the universe, "But this seductive new theory," says Brian Greene of Columbia University, "is also controversial. Strings, if they exist, are so small that there's little hope of ever seeing one."[11] Joseph Lykken, a researcher at Fermilab, adds, "If you can't test it in the way we test normal theories, then it's not science, it's philosophy, and that's a real problem."[11]

But even without a test, following the scientific method, there is still a sense among proponents that string theory is correct. Why? Professor S. James Gates Jr., a string theorist at the University of Maryland, says, "If string theory fails to provide a testable prediction, then nobody should believe it. On the other hand, there's a kind of elegance to these things, and given the history of how theoretical physics has evolved thus far, it is totally conceivable that some if not all of these ideas will turn out to be correct."[11]

Even without confirming experiments, Gates and others express a confidence (even without having a certainty) that string theory is true. This confidence, or intelligent intuition, comes from experience with theoretical physics – such that he can sense the 'elegance of these things.' He has lived with the accomplishments and directions of theoretical physics. Gates' confidence, probably trustworthy, is based on a relationship – not just with a person – but with a whole field of scientific inquiry. Gates' confidence probably is not that much different from Mott's ability to know how electrons think.

Yes, the good scientist as well as anyone should employ all the ways of knowing, using the one(s) most appropriate for the question at hand, not assuming that one is automatically superior to another. Yet too often this seems to have happened in an era where great emphasis has been placed on the scientific method. Try science first, today's conventional wisdom often tells us. And then only if science doesn't work use some other process of knowing, perhaps labeling a more relational process as 'mystical' or 'irrational' to designate its inferiority. We've all seen the old movie cliché, where the doctor comes into the waiting room and addresses the anxious family: "We've done all we can. I guess all we can do now is pray." As if prayer is a last resort, used only after science has done all it can. Rather, get the medical help quickly, indeed, but meanwhile pray and don't stop praying!

Faith is one form of relational knowledge, in fact it may be "most sublime form of non-scientific knowledge."[12] Scripture tells us that faith is much more than wishful thinking or desperate self-delusion: "Faith is being sure of what we hope for, and certain of what we do not see."[13] This 'being sure' and being 'certain' come from a relationship, not from a scientific proof (we'll discuss this further in Chapter 10). As philosopher Esther Meek says, "The person who knows God would rightly feel it inappropriate to say that their knowledge of him rests on a reasoned argument."[14]

Perhaps we still want a scientific proof of God's existence. Why hasn't he allowed us to find one? Why hasn't God made himself evident in a scientifically demonstrable way?

Why didn't he give us a more uncontestable sign about himself? Then, all this talk about science and religion would be unnecessary, wouldn't it? Or would it? Physicist Paul Davies writes,

"Suppose it could be demonstrated that life would be impossible unless the ratio of the mass of the electron to that of the proton was within 0.00000000001 percent of some completely independent number – say, one hundred times the ratio of the densities of water and mercury at 18 degrees centigrade. Even the most hard-nosed skeptic must surely be tempted to conclude that there was something fishy going on."[15]

Perhaps. Presbyterian minister Frederick Buechner asks the same question, but his conclusion is different. He writes,

"If God really exists, why in heaven's name does God not prove that he exists instead of leaving us here in terrible uncertainty? ... In some objectifiably verifiably and convincing way, we want God himself to demonstrate his existence ... and I have wondered sometimes what would happen if God did set about demonstrating his existence ...? Suppose, for instance, that God were to take the great dim river of the Milky Way as we see it from down here ... and were to brighten it up a little and then rearrange it so that all of a sudden one night the world would step outside and see ... written out in the heaven ... I REALLY EXIST."[16]

Buechner concludes that there would be an initial change of behaviors among believers and nonbelievers alike, but ultimately, on some future night, "a child would turn to his father, or maybe ... turn to God himself (and say), 'So what if God exists? What difference does it make?' ... and it would no longer make any difference." Buechner concludes that, while we all want proof of God's existence, what we really need to know is not

"...just that beyond the steely brightness of the stars there is a cosmic intelligence of some kind that keeps the whole show going, but that there is a God right here in thick of our day-to-day lives ... trying to get messages through our blindness as we move around down here in the muck and misery and marvel of the world. It is not objective proof of God's existence that we want but... the experience of God's presence. That is the miracle we are really after. And that is also, I think, the miracle that we really get."[17]

In these last two chapters we've briefly examined several ways of knowing, three objective ways and one subjective way. We've seen that for both science and faith, all these ways are valuable. We've seen that the scientific method fails us in fully knowing God because it explores only the reproducible. Both science and faith depend on the report of trustworthy witnesses and observing the effects, and both science and faith rely upon the relational way of knowing. As we have seen, this latter way surprisingly may be the most important way of guiding the three objective processes in science. While objective analysis may provide insights about God, relationship is the only way to truly know this God who has promised, not to give us all the answers but to never leave us or forsake us.[18]

One night, a small group from our church met at Tom's house to discuss science and religion. Tom was an accomplished mechanical engineer, and he led us in some good conversations, pondering questions like, "Can science prove or disprove God's existence?" "Are science and religion in conflict?" Many ideas, opinions and speculations bounced around the room. At the end of the evening, Tom accompanied us to the door. As I was leaving, he smiled and said to me, "It was a good discussion tonight, but you know, once you have a relationship with God, all this discussion about proving God's existence really isn't very interesting anymore."

4. How a Scientist Thinks About God

Many people have come to think that there is a conflict between science and faith. That somehow the answers they point to are in contradiction with one another. Some conclude that if you trust the results of modern science, then there is no need or rationale for having religious faith. Others conclude that if you are a person who believes in God, then you will naturally find yourself in conflict with the findings of modern science. How did it get to be that way? And is the conflict between science and religious faith real or false? We now turn to these questions.

A Brief History of the Relationship between Science and Faith

Despite the complexity and unresolved questions of modern science, contemporary culture has come to accept science as the primary source of answers in the world. It is popular to portray science as providing the answers to everything we seek. Science has become a kind of a god to some, commanding equal stature with the sovereign creator God. I remember a national church leader telling me a few years ago that he looked to the Bible as a source of guidance, only in a supporting role to the findings of science. How did science acquire this preeminent role, even among many religious people? Let's take a quick look at the history.

Until about 1700, the western world saw science as fitting perfectly into religion. In fact, almost all Europeans were Christians, and they accepted religious truth as coming down from God through scripture, experienced in the sacraments and revealed in the teachings of the church. Certainly there were bitter controversies within the Church, but there were few distinctions between the claims of science and religious faith. Most believers accepted the Bible as revealed truth from God. Certainly, scholarly investigation of nature was encouraged, but most accepted the theologian Anselm's famous view: "I believe in order to understand." Faith in God was the foundation upon which any scientific investigation was built. But by 1700, the popular view began to shift to something like, "I believe *because* I understand." [1] In a sense, biblical revelation was becoming replaced by man's reason as the vehicle for determining religious truth. These are two very different ways of encountering God. And these two different approaches to faith are very evident in the twentieth-first century American church.

Near the end of the seventeenth century, two shattering events occurred. In 1665, a young scholar named Isaac Newton, only 23, had just received his bachelor's degree from Cambridge University when an outbreak of the plague hit the London area. Young Newton fled to the countryside to escape the rampaging plague that was sweeping the cities. There, over a period of six months, Newton discovered and described the laws of classical mechanics—that is, all the relationships between motion, force and mass. Apparently the story that Newton's seminal work actually was inspired by his seeing a apple fall from a tree is true.[2] His work, published in 1687 in his landmark book *Principia Mathematica,* rocked the world. As Newton's biographer, James Gleick, says, "The *Principia* marked a fork in the road: thenceforth science and philosophy went separate ways. Newton had removed from the realm of metaphysics many questions about the nature of things – about what exists – and assigned them to a new realm, physics."[3]

Newton's equations beautifully described how long it would take an apple to fall from a tree as well as explaining all of the motions of the planets in the solar system. Physics seemed to have come to the point of being able to explain just about everything.[4] Even with the amazing scientific advances of the 20th century, no thinker has really surpassed the accomplishments of the reclusive Isaac Newton. In 1919, Albert Einstein, responding to the acclaim he was receiving for discovering the revolutionary laws of relativity, said, "Let no one suppose that the mighty work of Newton can really be superseded by this or any other theory. His great and lucid ideas will retain their unique significance for all time as the foundation of our whole modern conceptual structure in the sphere of natural philosophy."[5]

A few years after the publication of the *Principia*, in 1695, a friend of Newton's named John Locke, philosopher and a Christian, wrote an important book called *The Reasonableness of Christianity*, in which he argued that Christianity is the most plausible of all religions. But Locke did not believe that Christianity added anything of importance to what could just as easily be known from the correct use of reason. [6,7] He claimed that if you examine the order and moral character of the universe, you can deduce that God exists. Locke's arguments were seemingly not much different from the assertion of the Bible (e.g., Romans 1:20), but he carried it farther, saying in effect that we don't need revelation because we're intelligent enough on our own to deduce whether or not God exists. Buoyed by Newton's breakthrough discoveries in mathematics and physics and Locke's scholarly philosophy, the western world was now ready to embrace a new way of relating to religious faith.

The eighteenth century was a time of harmony between science and religious faith in the western world, and they were in mutual support until the 1800s, when two bombshell scientific discoveries revealed serious threats to the religious teaching of the day. The first threat came from geology, which cast doubt upon what many believers had come to accept as the age of the earth. In the 17th century, there was a certain Bishop James Ussher, who had examined all the genealogies in the Bible (he was probably one of the few Christians who ever actually studied all those tedious genealogies, you know: so-and-so begat so-and-so, who begat so-and-so, who lived 642 years, and so on). Ussher added up all those numbers, all the way back to the beginning, then added six more days from the Genesis account of creation (which Ussher assumed to be twenty-four hour days), and came to the conclusion that the earth was created in 4004 B.C. Ussher's conclusions came to be widely accepted by the Church and the culture in general, without much critical scrutiny.

But in the early 1800s the geologist Charles Lyell discovered fossils and geologic strata, and the conclusion from his study was inescapable: the earth is very, very old. In fact, Lyell reached the astounding conclusion that the earth is millions of years old, which if true (and it was hard to refute the geologic data), blew Ussher's conclusions out of the water. Of course, even Lyell greatly low-balled the best present-day scientific estimates of the age of the earth: *billions* of years old. The work of Lyell stood in startling contradiction to a literal reading of the creation account in Genesis (that is, assuming each 'day' of creation in Genesis to be an actual twenty-four-hour day). Some church authorities tried for awhile to refute the work of Lyell or just assert that his findings were wrong, but the new findings could not be easily dismissed.[8] Today there remains a small group of Christians who persist in arguing for a creation that occurred in six 24-hour days. But this literal interpretation of a "day" stands in opposition to scientific consensus.

Then an even greater challenge to religious teaching came in 1859, with Charles Darwin's publication of *The Origin of Species*, which introduced the theory of natural selection as an explanation of how species change over time. The Church is still rocking and reeling today from the impact of the theory of evolution, as the presupposed conflict of evolution versus creation is hotly argued. Only in the past decade have some scientists and religious thinkers begun to see that the ideas of evolution and creation may not be in conflict.[9]

Here's what one historian wrote about the relationship between science and religious faith near the end of the 19th century: "Physical science continued to pursue its own path unconcernedly, whereas theology, the science whose object is the dealings of God with man as moral being, maintained but a shivering distance, shouldered and jostled by the sturdy growth of modern thought and lamenting the hostility it encountered."[10]

At the beginning of the twentieth century, religion was assuming a less important role in the minds of many scholars, and the Church found itself on a slippery slope, poorly prepared to defend itself against new findings of science. Church leaders who tried to refute current scientific research were taking a beating.

By 1900 public confidence in science was high. It appeared to many, including intellectuals within the church, that science was appropriately replacing divine revelation (especially Scripture) as the way to understand the way God works. From the perspective of the twenty-first century, we can see it as naïve how many church leaders in the late 1800s so quickly abandoned the traditional teachings of the Church to embrace an understanding of God based on reason alone.[11]

21st Century Scientists Look at Faith

Scientists deal with objectivity. Just the facts. They look at the facts and they base their conclusions only upon concrete observation. This is what is conventionally believed about scientists, but it isn't always true.

While most scientists have a very high standard of ethics that values objectivity in research, most scientists I've known approach subjects of great personal importance like religious faith with pre-conceived bias, just like the rest of us do. As a physicist I have found that the general public does not realize this is so. They believe that scientists treat faith issues with the same high objectivity (and competence) that they apply to their science research. This often gives scientists more credibility in our culture, and we may tend to listen to their views on faith, even if they have little real background in that arena, in the same way we listen to movie stars teaching us about psychotherapy or foreign policy.

There are scientists who believe in God, there are scientists who are agnostic or atheists; but in my experience almost none of these people come to these positions based on what they learned from science, although sometimes they may try to convince you of that.

Let's consider two examples. Stephen Weinberg is a professor of physics at the University of Texas and Nobel Prize winner (1979) who has been a leading contributor to 21st century physics. Weinberg, an atheist, said:

> "As you learn more and more about the universe, you find you can understand more and more without any reference to supernatural intervention, so you lose interest in that possibility. Most scientists that I know don't care enough about religion even to call themselves atheists, and that I think is one of the great things about science. That it has made it possible for people not to be religious."[12]

Stephen Weinberg says he's looked at the scientific evidence, and he concludes that the evidence makes God unnecessary.

Yet many scientists do not concur. Here is the view of another physicist. Sir John Polkinghorne is a well-known theoretical particle physicist. He was president of the Queens

College at Cambridge University, and he is also an Anglican priest. He says: "The center of my faith lies in my encounter with the figure of Jesus Christ, as I meet him in the Gospels, in the witness of the church and in the sacraments. Yet at a supportive level there are also hints at God's presence which arise from our scientific knowledge."[13]

Two credible and respected scientists, two totally different conclusions. But is this surprising? Polkinghorne speaks for many believers, whether they are scientists or not, in stating that his faith comes not from scientific knowledge -- though he sees no inconsistency between his faith and science – but from the relational way of knowing discussed in Chapter 3.

The same is true for nonbelievers. Theologian and molecular biophysicist Alister McGrath states, "Most unbelieving scientists of my acquaintance are atheists on grounds other than their science; they bring those assumptions *to* their science rather than basing them *on* their science."[14]

My experience is that scientists tend to have about the same range of religious beliefs as does anyone else, and this conclusion indeed is supported by critical studies. Henry Schaefer, professor of chemistry at the University of California, Berkeley, records recent studies on the religious attitudes of scientists.[15] He reports one study by Alan Lightman, professor of physics at MIT, which concludes: "Indeed, contrary to popular myth, scientists appear to have the same range of attitudes about religious matters as does the general public." Schaeffer summarizes another study in 1988 by the professional scientific society Sigma Xi, based on the responses of over 3000 Ph. D. scientists, which finds that half the scientists participate in religious activities regularly, with 41% of them in church on a typical Sunday.

Whatever your view about God may be, you may not want to get into an argument with either Weinberg or

Polkinghorne about the existence of God *as proved by science,* because they will win the argument, but with two different conclusions! If you try to argue the existence or nonexistence of God from scientific principles alone, you are going to encounter someone who has a better command of science than you – but not necessarily a better spiritual understanding -- and faith in God will be difficult to defend. This is because the scientist will likely employ the objective ways of knowing in his argument, whereas knowing the truth of God also requires the subjective relational way of knowing, which is often difficult to put into words. There are better ways for spiritual persons to explain and articulate their faith, as we will see. To argue the existence of God with a scientist, using scientific arguments only, is sort of like deciding an argument with a great basketball star like Kobe Bryant by shooting free throws. It would be a huge mistake. Heaven forbid that you would be in an argument with Mr. Bryant, but if you are, don't try to settle it by shooting free throws!

Sometimes the Church has attempted to shoot free throws with Kobe Bryant by proclaiming Christian truth based upon its current understanding of scientific fact. History records how the Catholic Church humiliated itself in the 17th century in its clash with Galileo about whether or not the earth is the center of the universe. In the 1950s the Catholic Church asserted that creation had been proved, based upon the discovery of the Big Bang (this is discussed further in Chapter 7). But what happens if the Big Bang theory is one day disproved or modified such that this assertion is no longer plausible? Remember the concentric circles on page 9? It is risky business to attempt explanations that may reside in the outer circles using only the limited knowledge we have in the inner circles. The God that I believe in is known – not through attempted scientific proofs – but through the revelation of scripture, the witness of the church, the sacraments, and the inspiration of other believers.

We have heard the caution from St. Thomas Aquinas about building arguments for God on shaky ground. Another theologian who sought to apply reason to matters of faith, Anselm of Canterbury, lived in the eleventh century. Anselm also worried about trying to prove anything about God, using evidence that is flimsy and subject to change. He wrote,

> "I am afraid to handle the things that are too high for me. If someone thinks, or even sees, that I have not given him adequate proof, he may decide that there is no truth in what I have been saying, and not realize that in fact my understanding has been unable to grasp it." [16]

Nonetheless, I believe there are indications and hints in nature, especially as revealed in the 20th century, indicating that we are here because of a purposeful and loving creator. The Bible says, "From the time the world was created, people have seen the earth and sky and all that God has made. They can clearly see his invisible qualities - his eternal power and divine nature. So they have no excuse whatsoever for not knowing God." [17]

Maybe the reason I like these words is because they relate to my own life. I'd had a nominal faith in God since I was a child, probably as long as I can remember. I prayed occasionally, usually right before finals or asking a girl for a date, but most of the time I kept God in the background of my life. But in the early 1980s I experienced a deepening of my faith that was the beginning of a dramatic change in my whole life. It caught me by surprise, and I think oftentimes God does catch us by surprise. I was working as a research physicist, and my life had all the external trappings of success. I certainly thought I was doing pretty well. I loved my profession and I was climbing the professional ladder of recognition and responsibility. I had a nice home in Santa Fe, New Mexico, one of the loveliest places in the world. I had a lot of friends. But during that time I began to be aware of an emptiness in my life. I couldn't understand it. In retrospect, I would say -- and perhaps you've heard this term before – there was a God-shaped void in my life. I tried to fill that void, that emptiness, with all kinds of other things, but to no avail. I would find myself walking down the street, feeling great, and I would see a mother pass by with a little baby in a stroller, and I'd look at that little baby and be deeply moved in a way I couldn't understand. It was very strange behavior. Or I would see one of those incredible sunsets for which Santa Fe is famous, and all of a sudden tears would well up in my eyes. What was going on? It took awhile for me to understand that I was encountering God through his creation. I was seeing the beauty and the love around me, and it was pointing me toward the One who had provided these things. To paraphrase St. Paul, anyone ought to be able to see that there's a God just by going out and looking at the mountains or the twinkle in a child's eye. I finally got this.

Here we must be careful not to identify the beauty of nature or the rational order of the universe as God – this tendency has sometimes been popular in the scientific community[18] – but rather we see this beauty as *evidence* of a sovereign and creative God. Martin Luther said that if you could just comprehend a leaf—pick a leaf off the tree, and study it in detail—you'd fall to your knees in prayer to the One who created something so beautiful. That's what happened to me. In my case, I began to see that all along – even though I had kept God in the background – God was still there loving me through it all, waiting for me to come around, longing for a real relationship with me.

5. Let's Be Realistic

Let's now turn our attention to what you and I perceive as reality, as we begin to explore the surprising findings of physics in the past century. The Australian physicist and science writer Paul Davies talks about "naive reality" to describe our human perception of reality compared to what is really going on in nature – we are naïve because we naturally think we are grounded in realism (seeing is believing, right?), but the truth is that our senses barely give us a clue about the entities and processes all around us.

At the beginning of the 20th century, our culture had become comfortable and confident about its understanding of the physical world, based on our naive reality and the apparent victories of Newton's classical physics to describe just about everything. A scientist of that era might have said, "Isn't it beautiful how comprehensible and elegant the universe is!" At the beginning of the 21st century, just a hundred years later, a knowledgeable scientist might say, "Isn't it beautiful how complex and absurd and incomprehensible the universe is!" That's where we've come in a hundred years.

When I was a researcher at the Lawrence Livermore National Laboratory in California, I had the privilege of working with some of the most powerful lasers in the world. In fact, right now the most powerful laser in the world is preparing for experiments in energy research at Livermore, and it defies description. You have all seen lasers before, small devices used for bar-code scanners, pointers, and table-top experiments. But the laser just completed in Livermore – the National Ignition Facility – is as large as a football field, and it's at least ten stories high.[1] The National Ignition Facility will be used to produce conditions in the laboratory that replicate processes at the center of the sun, called nuclear fusion, and will hopefully demonstrate that nuclear fusion is a viable energy source for the future. If this scheme ever works – and there is considerable optimism, although there's a long way to go – the world will have cheap electrical energy that uses sea water as the fuel, while generating very little hazardous waste.

The physics underlying the laser fusion experiments is very complex, and I remember working with one theoretical physicist on this subject. I was designing experiments to understand how the super-intense light from high-powered lasers interacts with matter. We'd be addressing a particular physics question, but the experimental results were often difficult to interpret. My theoretical colleague said to me one day, "Jim, the problem with you experimentalists is that every time you shoot that laser at something, you may answer one question, but it raises ten new questions that we can't answer."

My colleague's comment was a profound truth that pointed to the complexity of reality that we are still struggling to grasp. One science commentator writes,

> "... when science runs out of questions, it would seem, science will come to an end. But there's no real danger of that. The highway from ignorance to knowledge runs both ways: As knowledge accumulates, diminishing the ignorance of the past, new questions arise, expanding the areas of ignorance to explore."[2]

As we begin our tour of the physical world, it is important to keep in mind that our scientific understanding is constantly evolving. We may look back and smile patronizingly at the relatively naïve understanding of physical reality a hundred years ago. Let's be aware that in another hundred years, people are likely to look at us in the same way.

Sizing Things Up – Limits to our Grasp of Reality

Before we engage some of the remarkable physics discoveries of the twentieth century, let's take a little personal inventory of our own ability to grasp reality. You think you are a 21st century rational being who has a pretty good grasp of reality? Well, with eyes wide open and feet firmly planted on the ground, let's take a look at the way things are, and let's just see how much we really do grasp.

Let's start simple, and just consider the size of things we can perceive with our senses, as a prelude to seeing that "the overarching lesson that has emerged from scientific inquiry over the last century is that human experience is often a misleading guide to the true nature of reality."[3] Begin by thinking about the smallest and the largest objects you and I can directly observe with our senses, not using devices like telescopes and microscopes. The smallest thing we can see without a microscope is something about the size of a speck of dust on the table, about one-thousandth of an inch in size. With an optical microscope you can see an object a few times smaller. With more advanced types of microscopes a whole new world of the very small opens up; yet even these complex devices can only extend our perception a short ways into the world of small objects, as we are about to see.

What is the largest object you can see? Quickly you might say, "The biggest thing I can see is the sun and the other stars." Well, that's true, but frankly we cannot grasp their true size. The sun is 800,000 miles in diameter, a hundred times the diameter of the earth yet only an average-sized star, but it is so far away from us that it really only appears to be a small quarter-sized disc, and the stars appear to be no larger than pinpoints. Because you can't travel to where the sun is located to perceive its enormous size, you have no grasp of how big it is, you have no grasp of how fast it's moving (in fact, our earth is moving 67,000 miles per hour relative to the sun right now), or really much of anything about it except that it provides a lot of warmth on a summer day. So I would say the biggest thing you can perceive is what you can see up close, maybe something like a mountain range or the extent of earth you can see from an airplane, perhaps 50 miles.

So, what are the largest and the smallest things that actually exist? The largest known object, of course, is the universe. And the universe is so big, I don't even know how to tell you how big it is. But I'll try to convince you of how far short we fall in trying to understand how huge it is. The known universe is about 10 billion light years across.* A light year is the distance light travels in one year, that is, about six trillion miles. So, the size of the known universe in miles is equal to a one with 21 zeroes behind it! We cannot grasp how large a number that is. So, let us try to imagine a miniature scale model of the universe and see if that helps.

I remember when I was in grade school and my teacher showed us models of the solar system made out of little Styrofoam balls on pieces of coat hanger, and you had the sun in the middle as the largest Styrofoam ball, and then there would be the earth, and Mercury and Venus and all the planets that revolved around the sun. I thought at the time, well that's kind of what the solar system must be like. Let's see. In our ultra-tiny scale model, let us assume that the earth is the size of a grain of sand, a grain of sand that you could place on the end of your finger and barely see. The earth is actually 8,000 miles in diameter, but we're shrinking it to the size of a grain of sand. In our scale model the moon would then be a somewhat smaller grain of sand -- about a quarter of the diameter of the earth --

---

* I refer to the 'known universe,' since it is possible the universe is actually much larger than 10 billion light years, if light from the most distant stars has not yet reached our earth. Nor can we rule out that there is more than one universe.

and it would be about an inch away from the earth, rotating around it. The sun, in this little scale model where the earth is a grain of sand, would be about the size of a tennis ball, and it would be about a hundred feet away. Pluto, the most distant object in our solar system, would only be about one mile away from the grain-sized earth. Already you can see how misleading my grade-school Styrofoam-ball model was. So this is our solar system: a tennis ball and a few grains of sand scattered over a square mile. A strange image, but at least we can grasp this.

Now let's ask, where would the next closest star be in this model? The star closest to our sun is Alpha Centauri, four light years away. If our little scale model were set up in Los Angeles, Alpha Centauri (also about the size of a tennis ball in our model) would be located in Boston. Now, remember Alpha Centauri is only four light years away. We know that there are stars over ten billion light years away! So, even our little scale model doesn't help us to grasp the enormity of the universe. You think you have a good perception of reality? You say, "Seeing is believing." But the truth is, while we can easily toss big numbers around, you and I have no grasp of just how vast our universe is.

Nor do we have a grasp of just how small the universe is. The smallest known objects in nature (and as we continue to learn more and more, we keep finding out there are smaller and smaller things!) are the particles that make up atoms. Only in the past hundred years, physicists learned that atoms, once thought to be the ultimate indivisible building blocks of matter, are comprised of smaller particles called electrons, protons, and neutrons. Then in the middle of the 20th century scientists discovered there are even smaller building blocks called quarks, which make up the protons, neutrons and many other subatomic particles. Although nobody has ever seen a quark, scientists are confident they exist, and the Nobel Prize for

Physics was won for their discovery. Now a growing community of physicists believes there are yet smaller entities called "strings" that may be the fundamental building blocks of all other particles, even the quarks. The size of a string is a matter of considerable debate, but most experts suggest they are no greater than 10^{-35} meters long – that's a one with 35 zeroes in front of it! So, a string is a trillion times a trillion times a million times smaller than the smallest things you can see with your eye (We'll talk more about strings in Chapter 9)! Even using sophisticated experimental techniques in scientific laboratories, such as the scanning tunneling microscope, we can only begin to resolve the positions of atoms – strings are trillions of times smaller yet, and even the most ardent proponent of string theory will confess that it is unlikely that we will ever be able to directly detect a string! And yet, everything – coffee cups, ravens, battleships, and your nose – is most likely composed of strings!

Let's summarize about the small and the big of things. The smallest things that we know are trillions of times smaller than what we can detect with even the most sensitive laboratory instruments. The largest things are a million times a billion times a billion times bigger than the largest things that we can see. (This number is comparable to the number of grains of sand in the Sahara Desert!) Now here's what's truly amazing: almost all of the objects around you at this very moment are either too large or too small for you and me to detect. It is justifiable to begin to lose confidence in your own ability to grasp reality.

Maybe these extreme numbers are beginning to boggle your mind, but let's keep going. As we continue to examine just how far short our grasp of reality falls, let's examine our practical intuition about the speed with which things happen. What are the fastest and the slowest motions that you and I can detect without special instruments? The fastest event we can resolve with our eye is about one thousandth of a second. The boxer Muhammad Ali used to claim he was so fast he could turn out the light switch in his bedroom and be in bed before the room was dark, but I think he was exaggerating a bit! We cannot see a speeding bullet fired from a gun because it's moving too fast. A bullet would take about a thousandth of a second to get across an ordinary room, but to our senses the puff of smoke from the gun barrel and the shattering of the wall on the far side of the room would seem instantaneous. Certainly there are high speed cameras, called framing cameras, that can take pictures that actually freeze a bullet in flight, and you've all seen those amazing pictures of a bullet as it passes through a pane of glass. But with our unaided eye, the fastest motions we can perceive are slower than about a thousandth of a second.

What is the longest duration event you can perceive? With our native senses, we can't perceive the motion of events that occur over much more than a few minutes. You can't see the motion of a flower blooming (unless you use time-lapse photography). You cannot see the sun moving across the sky; you have to wait a few minutes and then look again to realize that motion has taken place. You can't see a glacier move. Right now, all around us, metal is rusting, paint is peeling, rafters are sagging, and we're each getting older. Have you ever seen an acquaintance after five years and thought, "You know, I can't believe how Richard's aged" (or perhaps worse for our own egos: "I can't believe that Richard hasn't aged a bit!")? Yet, the aging process is taking place in each of us this very minute, and if our senses were finely enough tuned to detect slow events, we could see it (it's probably a blessing that this is not so).

So, the range of motions that we can see without using special cameras is from about one-thousandth of a second to maybe a thousand seconds. Maybe you could argue that there's a longer period of time we can observe directly -- maybe we are sensitive to changes over a hundred years, because of our memories, since that's about the maximum time that we can personally experience anything firsthand: "Isn't it amazing how the old hometown has changed!" But this won't make a lick of difference to the conclusion that our perception of slow events falls far short of reality.

The quickest known events taking place around you right now are the motions of and within the atoms of which all matter is composed. And they are occurring at least a thousand times a billion times faster that the shortest event you can sense. Amazingly, the vast majority of things happening around you right now are occurring that fast.

The longest event we know of is the age of the universe, about fifteen billion years, about a hundred million times longer than a human life.

Let's look at one final comparison between reality and what we perceive as reality. You know there's radiation all around us, but only a small range of this radiation is detectable by our eyes as visible light. Radiation is characterized by wavelength –the distance between the crests of the waves that make up the radiation, just like the distance between the peaks of the waves on the ocean would be the wavelength of that water wave. Light that is visible to you and me has wavelengths between about 15 millionths of an inch (very dark blue) to about 30 millionths of an inch (very deep red), and that's all you and I can see. We know there are shorter and longer wavelengths of radiation that we encounter every day, though we cannot see it. When your doctor takes an x ray, she is illuminating you with "light" that has a wavelength between a thousand and ten-thousand times shorter than what we can see. And when you turn on your microwave oven or tune in Rock 108 on your radio dial, you are using radiation with wavelengths that range between a million and a billion times longer than what you can actually see.

And yet, there are super-intense cosmic rays bombarding you right now that we did not even know about before twenty years ago with wavelengths trillions of times shorter than your dentist's x-ray! And there is also super-long-wavelength radiation flooding us right now that is a billion times longer than the waves from Rock 108. And no one knows from where either of these super-short or super-long waves comes.

Now if you think our little introduction to reality is not confusing enough, let's just think about space for a moment. At least that's something we understand – or do we? We live in a three-dimensional world, right? We are familiar with three-dimensional objects that have a width, a depth and a height. And if you study a little about relativity, you may argue that there are four dimensions, since we must include time as well. (We will see in Chapter 6 just how naive our intuition about time is.) The best thinking by the brightest physicists in the world today has produced a new idea called "string theory." One of the conclusions of string theory is that space does not look like our familiar four-dimensional impressions at all, but rather, has perhaps eleven dimensions. The best visualization of what a eleven-dimensional space looks like shows something that looks like a tangled ball of twine, although not even the most gifted scientist can envision such a space! 4 Eleven dimensions? Where are they? Why can't you see them? And you think you're a realist? You think you have an idea of what's going on? Do you think there might be a place for God in all of this beyond our meager grasp of reality?

Science has produced a great explosion of knowledge in the past hundred years, and much of this knowledge points to how much we still do not know and to just how naïve our understandings of science were at the beginning of the twentieth century. And that's why the whole topic of science and faith has been turned upside down as scientists and theologians both have emerged from a nineteenth century attitude of 'we've-got-it-all wrapped-up' confidence. As we ponder the facets of reality that we cannot see, consider what St. John writes: "No one has ever seen God. It is God the only Son, who is close to the Father's heart, who has made him known." [5] We should not expect to define, measure, prove or disprove God by our meager grasp of reality. There are hints of God in looking at creation, yet we are still naive in our grasp of what is real in the universe. Saying we have a grasp of reality, based on what we can see with our senses, is a bit like reading one word from the Library of Congress and claiming we are educated. We must acknowledge what St. Paul writes that "without a doubt the mystery of our religion is great."[6]

Though the world came to revere Isaac Newton's classical mechanics, Newton understood that his contributions to science barely scratched the surface and that indeed reality is so much more complex. Shortly before his death, Newton, a Christian, wrote:

> "I seem to have been only like a small boy playing on the seashore and diverting myself in now and then finding a smoother pebble or a prettier shell than ordinary, while the great ocean of truth lay all undiscovered before me."[7]

Raymond thought he understood reality too. And his naïve grasp of it nearly cost him his life. I remember the exact time and date very well. The research group was building a large physics research machine, a device called a pulsed-power machine, designed to produce super-high electric currents (a million times what one can draw from a household outlet!) for physics research. The construction of the machine was nearing completion, and it was now ready for its first test.

This was a special day, the first time the team would charge the new machine to its full capacity. Excitement was high as the machine slowly charged up, under the control of a computer. And then the moment came for the machine to discharge its stored electrical energy – everyone braced for the loud 'bang' that would accompany the intense discharge. But absolutely nothing happened. Everyone in the control room -- isolated from the machine behind inch-thick protective glass -- exchanged surprised looks. They knew there was a huge amount of electrical energy still stored in the machine, but it had not discharged in the way it had been designed. Something had gone wrong, and from where the team gathered behind the safety window the problem could not be diagnosed.

Stephen, the leader of the project and a bright electrical engineer, was quick to size up the situation. He informed the team that there was a failure in the system, and it would be necessary to go into the isolated room where the machine sat to diagnose what happened and fix it. It was a potentially dangerous situation, so Stephen and an experienced technician would go into the room, while everyone else was ordered to remain in the control room. And so Stephen and the technician – who knew how to manually discharge the machine -- unlocked the security doors and carefully stepped out into the room where the dangerous fully-charged machine awaited.

There was a summer student on the team, a young man named Raymond, 22 years old. He was a wet-behind-the-ears greenhorn, but he was full of enthusiasm, and he was excited and wanted to contribute – apparently so full of excitement that he didn't hear Stephen's caution to stay put, so full of excitement that he forgot the safety rules we had all been taught. Unbeknownst to the other team members – who were watching the device in anxiety through the thick glass window - - Raymond slipped out the back door of the control room and down the stairs to the lower level of this machine. Out of sight from the team, and in his zeal ignoring the DO NOT ENTER signs, he entered through the security doors, now unlocked, into the room where the fully charged machine was sitting. Raymond walked under the bottom portion of the huge device – out of sight from the others – and surveyed the device, looking for the cause of the malfunction. Almost immediately he saw it: a large copper conductor had been melted by the passage of a large electrical current, breaking the circuit and trapping the electrical energy inside the machine. Raymond was thrilled at his discovery. He pointed up to the melted copper bar and shouted, "I've found the problem!" And as he did, a purple arc of 20,000 volts came down into his hand, surged through his finger and through his right arm and the right side of his body, exiting to electrical ground through his right foot. Raymond's heart stopped, and he collapsed.

The other team members heard Raymond's call and realized suddenly where he was. They ran down to where Raymond lay crumpled on the floor, even though the nearby machine was still charged and very lethal. Stephen, the leader, comprehended immediately what had happened, and he was able to safely discharge the remaining energy from the machine. One of the team members, also an emergency medical technician, quickly began to apply CPR and got Raymond's heart beating again. Fortunately, Raymond had pointed to the machine with his right hand. If he had used his left hand, we were told later, the electrical current would have gone through his heart and killed him instantly. But Raymond survived, suffering only a burn on his foot that would eventually heal. Despite all our safety training and our well-executed safety procedures, a colleague and friend had almost been killed.

The accident also destroyed the morale of the team. Stephen's team had been a gung-ho, energetic group, but its spirit was now broken. For weeks afterward, most of us could do little more than stare at the wall. No one seemed to care whether the research program succeeded anymore. We could only think about what had happened to Raymond.

Finally, in an attempt to help the team, I accompanied Stephen and two of his team members to meet with one of the senior leaders for the whole institution. Perhaps he could say something to rekindle our spirits. Ethan welcomed us into his office and invited us to sit down. He listened carefully as I explained how the team was struggling. The team members then spoke and told Ethan of their suffering.

Ethan leaned back in his chair, considering our story. Then he said, "I recall another man who suffered." He paused, and we were all silent for awhile. He didn't elaborate on those few words, and it wasn't necessary because it was clear he was referring to Christ, the one who suffered on our behalf, the one who forgives, the one who heals, the one who makes all things new. Although we talked about many other things during that meeting, it was those simple words that helped to start the team back onto a path of recovery in their careers and in their lives.

We had been grounded in a reality built on an understanding of physics and engineering. But through our brokenness, we were led into a greater reality, one that is not naïve but is deep and true.

6. Just a Matter of Time

Time -- which we often don't seem to have enough of, but sometimes we have too much of, 'time to kill' – is a mysterious thing. We take time for granted, since it's always there, yet we are aware that we are given a finite allotment of it in our lives, and we often regret most our wasting of time. We are so immersed in time that it is hard for us to even wonder about what 'time' actually is. The twentieth century did not make the concept of time easier for us to grasp. Instead, it challenged our naïve reality about time with startling new discoveries that perhaps have only deepened the mystery. Let us then examine the two radical discoveries about time that the twentieth century revealed, for time is of the essence.

Einstein and his shocking discovery

The revolution in understanding time started with Albert Einstein. In fact, you cannot have a grasp of what happened in early 20th century physics and how revolutionary it was without talking about Einstein. Einstein's contributions to twentieth century science are so significant that *Time* magazine selected Albert Einstein as the most important person in the world of the 20th century. That FDR and Gandhi were second and third, respectively, should give you some idea of the importance of Einstein's contributions. Albert Einstein was number one. Along with Galileo and Newton, Einstein may be one of the three most influential physicists who ever lived.

And yet Einstein's early days were anything but remarkable. Albert Einstein was born in Germany in 1879 to an artistic mother and a father who was a rather practical small-business man. Einstein was Jewish, but his parents were agnostic, and so he received little religious upbringing.[1] It is true that young Albert did not speak his first words until he was three. At the age of five, Einstein's family moved to Munich, away from their small home town, and they enrolled him in a Catholic school because that's where they thought he could get a good education. Albert was an unexceptional, average student. In fact, it is reported that Einstein's headmaster even told his parents that it was unlikely that Albert would ever amount to anything (This lesson should be great encouragement for all of us who have felt like failures on occasion).

At age ten young Albert transferred to another school, and he didn't fit in well there. However, he apparently became interested in science around this time, due to his uncle, an electrical engineer, who would talk to him about mathematics and science. Einstein would later remember how he'd been thinking about many of his physics problems since he was about age thirteen. Maybe he didn't speak until he was three because he couldn't find anyone intelligent enough with whom to converse.

When Einstein was fifteen, his parents moved to Italy, leaving Albert at the school in Munich, where he was not happy. He was expelled from school for disruptive behavior and being disrespectful to teachers. He then tried to get admitted to a prestigious technical school in Switzerland, but he failed the entrance exam. Finally in 1896, at age seventeen, Einstein was admitted to the technical school, where he graduated in 1900. Though he was recognized as bright, he was regarded as just a typical student. Einstein became a Swiss citizen, but he had physical limitations. He suffered from varicose veins and flat feet, and so the military didn't want him either.

It was around this time that Albert fell in love with a young Serbian woman (and fellow physics student) named Mileva. When Mileva became pregnant, a scandal between the families erupted, and so Albert and Mileva were married. Mileva was a pretty woman, and she and Albert had two children. However, they were never close and were later divorced. Albert would later marry his cousin, with whom he also was not close. Amidst all of this turmoil Albert Einstein finally earned his Ph.D., but the best he could do following graduation was to get a job in the patent office in Bern, Switzerland, in about 1903.

Up to this point we see a portrait of a capable but unexceptional person. A person who some of us might say got off on the wrong foot; we might even brand him a troublemaker, an unexceptional kid, so don't expect too much out of him. So why did *Time* magazine select Albert Einstein as the most important person in the world of the 20th century? It was because of what he began to do while he was working in that patent office at the age of 26, and what he did shook the very foundations of science.

In less than one year, in 1905, Albert Einstein wrote three independent papers, each of which was worthy of an individual Nobel Prize. Einstein finally did win the Nobel Prize in 1921 for his 1905 paper on the photoelectric effect, which laid the groundwork for some aspects of quantum mechanics. He also wrote a paper on Brownian motion and statistical mechanics, which provided the theoretical foundation for the invention of the laser over fifty years later. And Einstein's third paper, the most famous, was on the theory of special relativity. He never won a prize for his discovery of relativity, however, because the work remained controversial for so many years. Even experts just could not grasp that Einstein's radical theory could possibly be true, and in fact there were debates about Einstein's theory even up into the latter half of the 20ᵗʰ century. Though his theory has turned out to be an important cornerstone in our understanding of reality, for a long time the world didn't quite know what to do with this Person of the Century.

Einstein's special theory of relativity completely overturned our whole idea of time. And even today it's hard to grasp, because we tend to think of time as an absolute flowing unalterable reality, "time like a river flows," and we derive a certain security in knowing that somewhere precise atomic clocks can tell us the absolute time to within tiny fractions of a second. What Einstein showed is that there is no such thing as absolute time, but rather time is dependent on how fast you are traveling. And so time is truly only a relative thing.

The Theory of Relativity

As we attempt to better understand time, let's see how you and I intuitively grasp relativity. Imagine two cars driving down the highway, the first one traveling at 45 mph and the other car traveling at 40 mph, so to the passenger in the slower car, it appears that the faster car is going only 5 mph, right? 45 minus 40 equals 5. In fact, if they were going the same speed, the drivers could look out the window and see each other just sitting there. If they didn't notice the countryside flying by, they might not even be aware that they were moving at all, would they? One driver could have a conversation with the other driver (I've been behind cars doing just that!) We all can grasp this situation; it's called classical relativity, and it's the way we understood moving objects until Einstein came along. Einstein began his theory by considering the speed of light. We know that light travels very fast. In fact, it travels 670 million miles per hour, so fast that if you sent out a little pulse of light right now -- and you had an arrangement of mirrors that could steer the pulse around the earth -- your pulse of light would travel around the earth nearly eight times in one second.

So light is incredibly fast, but that's not the surprising part. What Einstein assumed in his theory, and it turned out to be right, is that no matter how fast you're traveling, the speed of light relative to you is always the same constant speed of light. To understand what that means, let's go back to our picture of the two cars. Imagine one car is traveling at the speed of light. Now don't try this in your car, because the speeding ticket you would get (if the police could catch you) would be astronomical. Even in my hometown of Los Angeles, where people drive fast, going 670 million miles an hour on the interstate is just not acceptable! Now imagine the first car is going the speed of light, and the second car – a tad slower -- is going half the speed of light. Our intuition, based on classical relativity, would say that if this car was going half the speed of light, when the driver looked out the window at the faster car, it would be going half the speed of light relative to her.

Makes perfect sense, but Einstein said no, that's not correct at all. If the driver of the slower car is going half the speed of light and looks at the faster car, she sees it moving ahead of her at the speed of light. It doesn't matter how fast the slower car is going, even if that car is traveling very close to the speed of light, say 660 million miles per hour, and the driver looks out the window at the one going 670 million miles per hour, what he will see is not a car moving ahead at 670 million minus 660 million miles per hour (that is, ten million miles per hour), but rather moving at the full speed of light. Well, that doesn't make any sense at all, does it? But that's what Einstein claimed, and it provided the explanation to some puzzling physics experiments performed around that time.[2]

A physicist would express Einstein's assertion about light by saying that the speed of light is the same in all frames of reference. No matter how fast you're going, something else going the speed of light is always going the speed of light relative to you.

If you start working out the mathematics (actually relatively simple algebra), you will find out some very amazing things are implied by this statement about the speed of light. One prediction is that as your speed increases, your mass increases. (That's always been my argument against jogging, by the way.) But this amazing prediction is true. In fact the theory states that you can never achieve the speed of light because the mass of an object not only increases as you travel faster and faster, but it becomes infinite as you approach the speed of light. So to accelerate an object up to the speed of light would ultimately require an infinite force. This reality has been demonstrated in many particle accelerators like the ones at Fermilab in Illinois, and the linear accelerator at Stanford University. Mass increases when speed increases. We know that this is true.

Another prediction of Einstein's theory is that the length of an object contracts as speed increases. But perhaps most surprising of all is the prediction of special relativity that time slows down when speed increases. Let's look at the two speeding cars again. If one car is going near the speed of light and the other car is going slower -- and we place a clock in each automobile and ask the drivers to compare their clocks when they stop later at the McDonalds ten million miles up the road -- the drivers would find that they have two different times registered on their clocks. Time passes differently depending on how fast you're going. That doesn't make any sense to us, but it's absolutely true. Perhaps Yogi Berra's explanation will help. When asked to explain the theory of relativity, he replied that the theory of relativity states that time always slows down when you're with your relatives. Now we're getting a handle on this, right?

The Amazing Story of Ann and Betty

So far, you may shrug and say that this talk about relativity is some abstract physics thing that doesn't really involve us. Well, I want to introduce you to a couple friends of mine, Ann and Betty. Now Ann and Betty are identical twins, aged 25 (but they could be any age for the sake of this example). Ann has always been a little bit of a wilder girl than Betty. So the opportunity came up for Ann to go into a space ship and travel into outer space at a speed near the speed of light, and she said, "Hey, why not?" So Ann went for a relativistic spin one afternoon, while Betty stayed at home on earth. Now both Ann and Betty had accurate clocks with them and they measured the passage of time during Ann's trip. It turned out to be a long trip. In fact, Betty, sitting at home on earth, measured the passage of 25 years. Will that sister of mine ever get home?

So by the time Ann actually did return, Betty was now 50 years old. She had married and had four children in the interim, but that's another story. Now Ann had accelerated up to nearly the speed of light out into space, slowed down, turned around, re-accelerated back to earth, and finally made it back to earth. During that time, the theory of special relativity says that time had slowed down so much that her clock said only six months had passed. Now the question I want to ask you is this. What did Ann and Betty see when Ann stepped off the space ship? According to Einstein, Ann was twenty five and a half years old, while Betty was fifty! Is this possible?

Do you believe this? Is Betty really almost 25 years older than Ann now, or are they the same age they were in the beginning? The truth is, they would indeed be different ages. Betty would be 50 years old, and Ann would be only 25 years old and six months (not to mention being the owner of an incredible number of frequent flyer miles). Now you might say, if that is true, isn't this the secret to living forever? You just go out and travel at the speed of light and you could stay young for a long time! But, of course, there's always a catch, because Ann really only experienced the passage of six months. She didn't get any extra time; she just got shifted in time relative to what was happening on earth. So when she came back, she hadn't had all the 25 years of living that Betty had.

So, modern science has determined that time is not a universal absolute quantity that passes the same for everybody. And I'm not talking about mere perception like the wisecracking comic said: "When I'm with my girlfriend, time stands still. She has a face that would stop a clock!" (from Cole Porter's *Anything Goes*). Time actually depends on how fast you are traveling.

Of course, no one has traveled (nor will they) in a light-speed space ship, no matter how many Star Trek episodes you might have seen. However, the special theory of relativity has indeed been proved. Here's one proof. If we turned on a Geiger counter, we would immediately see an indication of radioactive particles due to cosmic rays from space, interacting with atoms in our atmosphere to create highly energized particles that then rain down to the surface of the earth, where we can measure them. One such charged particle is called a muon, which is a little heavier than an electron. It can easily be detected with a Geiger counter. Now muons are very unstable particles and decay away in only about two millionths of a second. That's not very unusual, but here's the interesting part. Muons are produced at the top of the atmosphere, around a hundred kilometers above the surface of the earth. Even if they could travel at the speed of light (remember they cannot even reach that speed), they would travel less than one kilometer before decaying away.

So, why are we able to detect cosmic muons at the surface of the earth? The answer is a demonstration of special relativity at work. It's because those muons are traveling so fast that in their frame, they are just like Ann in her spaceship. In their frame of reference, time slows down, so the muon experiences a time of less than a microsecond before making it all the way to the earth's surface, whereas we watching them come down would say that perhaps hundreds of microseconds have passed. So, this is a proof that time actually does slow down for speeding objects.

Researchers have also studied the difference in times measured by very accurate atomic clocks, both stationary and aboard aircraft. At aircraft speeds, far slower than the speed of light, the effect of relativity is very small. Yet, with the high precision of atomic clocks, a small shift in times due to special relativity has been clearly observed.[3]

This is all pretty amazing stuff, and it totally overwhelmed the intellectual establishment of Einstein's day. In fact, Nobel Prize winners traveled around the country arguing against Einstein for years – they couldn't grasp that his theory could be true, and that's why he never won the Nobel Prize for this discovery. They said in essence, "This is stupid, it violates our experience, it can't possibly be right." Naïve reality.

Time's Up

Okay, time's up, pencils down. How do you react to such a startling discovery as special relativity? Head buried in the sand about it? Of course, if that's your position, you're in the good company of many of the prominent (but wrong!) scientists of the twentieth century.

What are some of the things that faith traditions would say about this radical discovery about time? Here's where we've got to be a little careful, because there are some extreme viewpoints that assert that modern discoveries like relativity and nuclear fission are actually predicted in the Bible. Such claims require stretches in Biblical interpretation I find incredulous. Let's be cautious with such statements, remembering that the Bible was not intended to be a predictor of science and technology. However, the Bible does suggest that we should not be surprised at new developments such as special relativity. About conventional wisdom it says: "It is written, I will destroy the wisdom of the wise and of the discerning I will thwart."[4] In other words, when you come at issues out of your own human intuition and conventional wisdom -- and this is a good message for all those people who were opposing Einstein -- be careful! You may end up with egg on your face. And that's what happened to much of the scientific establishment when they confronted Einstein.

As mentioned above, the purpose of the Bible is not to comment on science. In the book of Genesis, the account of creation is only 31 verses, compared to 209 verses describing God's relationship with Abraham. Where is God's emphasis? It's on his relationship with human beings; it's not to give a detailed explanation of how he created the universe. At the conclusion of St. John's Gospel, he does not write: "These [*the Gospels*] are written that you would understand the secrets of the universe." No, rather he says they're written "that you may come to believe that Jesus is the Messiah, the Son of God, and that through believing, you may have life in his name."[5] When new scientific discoveries are made, believers in God should marvel at them and thank God for allowing humans finally to be able to learn more about this beauty. There is no reason for people of faith to respond out of defensive fear and denial, and they must be very careful about attempting to explain scientific discoveries from religious doctrine, which "sees through a mirror dimly."

Relativity is exciting, wonderful stuff and has tremendous implications. Yet, even this special theory of relativity is a naive theory, because it is valid only for unchanging speeds. In order to treat changing speeds (which is called acceleration) and the geometry of Newton's classical laws, the theory of relativity becomes much more complex and requires a new level of sophistication, called *general relativity*, a topic that Einstein devoted much of the rest of his life to articulating and which has become a chief theoretical cornerstone in understanding how the universe behaves.

Why should we care how God has made time to behave? Why should we become upset when our naïve sense of reality needs overhauling? From the Book of Isaiah, the Lord speaks: "Does a clay pot ever argue with it's maker? Does the clay dispute with the one who shapes it, saying 'stop, you are doing it wrong?'" In other words, the theory of relativity can't be right because that's not the way we've ever experienced it before; stop, God, you are doing it wrong! The prophet Isaiah continues,

"This is what the Lord, the creator and holy one of Israel says: 'Do you question what I do? Do you give me orders about the work of my hand? I am the one who made the earth and created people to live on it. With my hand I stretched out the heavens; all the millions of stars are at my command.'"[6]

When we react in fear to modern scientific findings, we are not demonstrating faith in God, but rather, I suspect, faith in our naïve reality.

As we think about the implications for 20th century physics on the belief in God, it is interesting to consider how St. Paul argued for the existence of God. A good place to start is with his first visit to the city of Corinth, around 51 A.D., about twenty years after the resurrection. Paul was a formidable scholar. He studied under the greatest high priest of the Pharisees. He was highly educated and articulate. Today, even in secular universities his letters are studied as great literature. If you read Paul's letters in the original Greek, you find they are very complex. He even invented new words. If anyone could defend himself in an intellectual argument, it probably was Paul. He could have given Kobe Bryant a run for his money in shooting free throws. He was a brilliant man. Yet it was not upon his intellect that Paul exclusively relied.

At the time Paul first visited Corinth, which is located on the southern tip of Greece, it was a huge city of perhaps 500,000 people, the size of modern-day Denver. A busy commercial and cosmopolitan city. A perfect place for Paul to go head to head with pagan Roman culture and convince its people about God. Well, is that what Paul did? Let's see what Paul actually says he did. He writes (with my comments inserted in italics):

> "When I came to you, brothers and sister, I did not come proclaiming the mystery of God to you in lofty words or wisdom." (*In other words, I could have done that, because I am probably more articulate than you, but I decided not to do it*). "For I decided to know nothing among you except Jesus Christ, and him crucified. And I came to you in weakness and in fear and in much trembling. My speech and my proclamation were not with plausible words of wisdom, but with a demonstration of the Spirit and of power, so that your faith might rest not on human wisdom (*that is, not on the cleverness of my logical arguments*) but on the power of God."[7]

Paul indicates that believers in God (scientists and non-scientists alike) will have more impact in explaining their faith by speaking to others humbly from their hearts and minds, without arrogance and attempts to impress with articulate arguments. In other words, long complicated scientific arguments about the complexity of the universe will be less effective in discussing your faith than just telling your story.

I do not believe that most people come to faith in God through the process of scientific proof or through someone else sharing rationale that is based on science. That doesn't mean that believers reject knowledge and stand blindly opposed to scientific discovery. The most amazing thing in all the universe is the human brain. When someone looks at the vastness of the night sky through a telescope, "the most significant thing in the known universe is still immediately behind the eyes of the astronomer." [8] Galileo was more direct: "I do not feel obliged to believe that the same God who has endowed us with sense, reason, and intellect has intended us to forgo their use."[9] God gave us a magnificent brain and he expects us to use it. Yet ultimately, God is going to be known to us through relationship. My friend Harold could never grasp that relationship.

Harold was a very bright theoretical physicist, and he was also an ethical and delightfully funny guy. He was a scientific leader, with great analytical skills, and he was always curious about faith. Harold knew that I was a Christian, so occasionally he would come to me and ask about religious faith. Harold wanted to see evidence of God. He wanted somehow to grasp it intellectually, and he wasn't really very interested in making a commitment without data to back it up. Harold saw the evidence of faith in other people, including me and many others around him, but he just couldn't experience it for himself. He sensed that if he could just overcome his questions and his skepticism, there was something wonderful awaiting him. Now twenty years have passed and Harold still hasn't come to any conclusions about God. He is still struggling with his intellectual barriers, and I'm convinced he's missing out on the greatest relationship of his life. When we consider the romantic relationship between a man and a woman, isn't it good that we don't approach it by doing some interminable analysis like Harold was doing in trying to come into a relationship with God – holding out for some final conclusion where everything is evaluated on a spreadsheet and numbers have to be added up before you decide whether or not you're going to fall in love.

Time did not help Harold understand God's love for him.

7. Just a Matter of Time, Part 2

A Second Shocking Discovery: The Big Bang

While the scientific world was still hotly debating Einstein's theory of relativity, the second big shock about time was already unfolding. During the 1920s a gifted astronomer named Edwin Hubble spent much of his time behind large telescopes, making careful measurements on distant stars. Surprisingly, everywhere he looked, stars seemed to be rapidly moving away from earth. In 1929 Hubble made the startling announcement to the world that the universe is expanding. His discovery led to the inevitable conclusion of a Big Bang, a cosmic explosion at a point in time that set the whole universe into motion. This discovery was every bit as controversial as Einstein's and was hotly contested for decades. The discovery of the Big Bang has stimulated, perhaps more than any other event in the twentieth century, the dialogue between science and religion.

We must realize that the early cultures -- the Greeks (including Aristotle himself), far Eastern cultures, and the Mayans -- believed that the universe was static, eternal, and infinite. This was also the widely held view among western cultures until the mid-twentieth century. Some people thought the universe might be cyclic in some way, because they saw the seasons on earth, but believed it was basically infinite in extent. Yet, for a long time mathematicians and physicists had a problem with calculating the properties of an infinite and eternal universe, even though they believed that was the case. If the universe is infinite in extent and the stars are not moving, the amount of starlight calculated to be falling on the earth should make the night sky as bright as day. Obviously this is not true. Perhaps this was just a minor problem. But, as has often been the case in physics, small discrepancies between experiments and theory give hints of important underlying physical reality. Fortunately for us, scientists like Einstein and the founders of quantum mechanics did not ignore small discrepancies, and their pursuit of reconciliation between experiment and theory led to the founding of totally new fields of physics.

Galileo and Isaac Newton also believed that the universe was eternal and infinite, and that view persisted in the scientific community right up until Hubble's amazing discovery.[1] In fact, the astrophysicist Sir Fred Hoyle, who coined the term "Big Bang," maintained that the universe was infinite until his death in 2001.

The controversy about the reality of a Big Bang was put to rest only in 1965, when investigators discovered a very low-temperature background everywhere in the universe, clearly the residue of an expanding explosion.[2]

The Big Bang discovery indicates that the whole known universe was produced by a violent explosion some 14 billion years ago,[3] expanding from an initial microscopic size -- in fact it came out of nothing! One question people often ask about the Big Bang is, "What was going on ten minutes before the Big Bang?" This is a meaningless question because scientists now believe that both time and space only came into being at the Big Bang, another challenge to our naïve reality. There was no "before" in a temporal sense, nor was there a vast empty space just waiting for the Big Bang to fill. So, there's no sense of time before that moment of creation 14 billion years ago. In other words, time had a beginning.

We can't intuitively grasp what it means for space and time not to exist, but that's exactly what St. Augustine proposed in the early 400s. Speaking to God, he wrote:

"You are the maker of all time. If, then, there was any time before you made heaven and earth, how can anyone say that you were idle? You must have made that time, for time could not elapse before you made it. But if there was no time before heaven and earth were created, how can anyone ask what you were doing 'then'? If there was no time, there was no 'then.'" 4

This is pretty exciting stuff for believers, and it is tempting to reflect upon the theological implications of the Big Bang. Yet we must approach this discovery with caution. It's tempting to say "Aha, the Big Bang proves creation." In fact, in 1951 Pope Pius XII proclaimed, "Science has provided proof of the beginning of time; hence, creation took place in time. Therefore, there is a creator; therefore God exists."5 I believe the Pope's conclusion is correct (but because of my faith in God, not because of science). However, I worry that the Church has now placed its argument for creation, for there being a creator, upon a newly-interpreted scientific discovery. This Big Bang is so complicated and many of our insights into the expanding universe still so tentative, we should not rule out the possibility that in a hundred years scientists may interpret the origin of universe in a totally different way. Indeed we should not forget the caution from C. S. Lewis, the 20th century Oxford scholar:

"Science is in continual change, and we must try to keep abreast of it. For the same reason, we must be very cautious of snatching at any scientific theory which, for the moment, seems to be in our favour. We may *mention* such things; but we must mention them lightly and without claiming that they are more than 'interesting.' Sentences beginning 'Science has now proved' should be avoided."6

The Church's pronouncement about the Big Bang should make believers nervous, when we consider the erroneous position the Church took in 1615 at Galileo's inquisition: "The view that the earth is not the center of the universe is philosophically false and at least erroneous in belief."[7] Believers in God do not need to rest their arguments for God upon scientific discovery. There's a different approach that's much more powerful and effective; that is to tell people the good news about God's love for them. That's what I suspect they really need to hear anyway.

Yet, the implications of the Big Bang are very tantalizing for believers in God. It's tempting to associate the current belief of scientists that there was a definite moment when the universe was created with the creation story from Scripture. Keeping all the cautions in mind, we find the results of Big Bang research to be, as Lewis would say, quite 'interesting.'

One of the discoverers of the background radiation that confirmed the Big Bang and recipient of the 1978 Nobel Prize for physics was Arno Penzias. Penzias said, "The best data we have (concerning the Big Bang) are exactly what I would have predicted, had I nothing to go on but the five books of Moses, the Psalms, and the Bible as a whole."[8] Yet, we must be aware that arguments have been developed for why the Big Bang does not necessarily imply a creator[9] and that alternative explanations for the Big Bang (other than implying a creator) are being sought.[10] We further note that the doctrine of creation is less concerned with the beginning of the universe than *why* we are here and God's *ongoing* role in his creation. John Polkinghorne points out,

> "... big bang cosmology is not a scientific validation of the existence of a Creator, since God's role is not merely initiation but sustaining, holding the universe in being throughout history, whether the history is finite or infinite in duration."[11]

So, the exciting news here is that God's work in the universe is not just about getting everything started, but about its ongoing development. This includes the fate of the cosmos and also the fate of your life.

A Beginning of Time? Eternal Life?

Sure, it's tempting for believers in God to try to relate what their faith traditions say about time with recent discoveries. But is this a good idea? For one thing, does this not do injustice to all those generations of believers who accepted the biblical creation story without any supporting scientific data? Remember the story of the apostle Thomas? He's the one who demanded proof that Jesus had been raised from the dead. Then when Jesus appeared before Thomas, Jesus told him, "Because you have seen me, you have believed; blessed are those who have not seen and yet have believed."[12] Similarly, many faithful generations have believed and trusted in God without requiring supporting evidence from science. A deeper concern is that relating the claims of an ancient faith to current scientific ideas that may change is risky business; recall C. S. Lewis' guidance in the last section to avoid any statement that begins with the words, "Science has now proved ..."

Yet, in spite of complex issues surrounding the connection of the Big Bang with the biblical accounts of creation, the Scriptures are indeed remarkable in indicating a definite beginning to the universe, a beginning of time, and a place of eternity somehow outside of time. The Bible begins with, "In the beginning, God. . . ," implying that at creation there was a purposeful presence intent upon creative action.

The apostle John wrote, "In the beginning was the Word."[13] This is a very familiar Bible passage, but when you consider the words carefully you realize how astounding (and perhaps confusing) it is. John says that "in the beginning" there was already something that pre-existed the beginning. And that something was the Word, who is Jesus. Amazingly, this astounding pronouncement was written by a first-century fisherman.

In another amazing passage,[14] the Pharisees are confronting Jesus:

> "Are you greater than our father Abraham, who died? The prophets also died. Who do you claim to be?" And Jesus said, "Your ancestor Abraham rejoiced that he would see my day. He saw it and was glad."

Such talk about a patriarch now dead for over a thousand years astounded the Pharisees, as it would us. How could this man Jesus make such claims?

> Then the Jews said to Jesus, "You are not yet fifty years old, and you have seen Abraham?" And Jesus said to them, "Very truly, I tell you, before Abraham was, I am."

Now Jesus didn't use these words because he flunked eighth-grade English. No, this statement by Jesus is part of the mystery of our faith. It goes back to the burning bush, when Moses, encountering God, asks, "What is your name?" And the voice of God says, "I am who I am."

God speaks in the present tense about himself. God seems to be in the eternal present, where there is no distinction between past or future.

The idea of eternal life begins to make more sense as we consider these texts. But let's not get too confident about our understanding about something that is so incomprehensible as the possibility of eternal life. Believers in God may not be able to make sense of it, but they embrace this mystery with hope because of the reports of believable witnesses. The idea of eternal life is mentioned, by the way, 44 times in the New Testament, so this is more than a topic of minor interest in the Christian faith tradition. Eternity is a prominent theme in the New Testament, too recurrent and too radical and too profound for a group of cowardly fishermen and tax collectors to have fabricated. The most familiar reference to eternal life, of course, are the words of Jesus in John 3:16: "For God so loved the world that he gave his only Son, so that everyone who believes in him may not perish but have eternal life." But there are many other amazing statements about Jesus as the unchanging, eternal One; for example, "Jesus Christ is the same yesterday, today and forever."[15]

The Bible tells us that we are created in God's own image. Perhaps there is something of the eternal in us, even as we live our day-to-day lives in mortal bodies. C. S. Lewis wrote,

> "Do fish complain of the sea for being wet? Or if they did, would that fact itself not strongly suggest that they had not always been, or would not always be, purely aquatic creatures? Notice how we are perpetually *surprised* by time. ('How the time flies! Imagine John being grown up and married! I can hardly believe it!') In heaven's name, why? Unless, indeed, there is something in us which is *not* temporal."[16]

Fish are not surprised about being wet because they were meant for the sea. We are surprised by time, because we are creatures most at home outside of time, in eternity. We are meant for it.

Admitting that our intuition about time is yet naïve, let me share with you a simple image of what time and eternity may be like. The following model is simple, but then so is my grasp of time. Imagine that you are sitting in a compartment of a train car (like in a scene from one of those old movies from the 1940s). There is one small window from which you can survey the countryside through which the train is traveling. All you can see of the surrounding landscape is what you can see out that narrow window. You can't see the countryside that lies ahead, nor can you see the countryside you've passed, although you may have a memory of what you saw. Time is like the moving train, with the narrow view from the car being the present, the unseen but remembered countryside behind you the past, and the unseen countryside ahead being the future.

There's a future ahead of you, and there's a past behind you that still exists – it's real, but we cannot experience it, because we are stuck in the train car clickety-clacking along the track. Maybe to be in eternity is to simply get off the train, where the whole span of what we call time is now available to us – the eternal present. Maybe God is outside the train, where he can see the past, and he can see the future. Maybe when we die, we meet him there.

But there's more. Somehow, this God who can be outside of time, values time greatly. He invented it. And he is able to function within the realm of time too, sustaining and guiding his creation through time, knowing the number of hairs on our heads and holding us in the palm of his hand.

This simple picture might help us understand another common question about time. Some people ask, "If God already knows the future, doesn't that mean I have no independent will? What's the use of trying, if the result of my life has already been determined?" Have you ever heard that question raised? Well, let me ask you: Do you remember what you were doing yesterday? Yesterday, you made some decisions, didn't you? Yesterday, God was present with you to nurture and guide you, and you could freely decide to accept or reject his assistance. But today, you know the consequences of actions you took yesterday. You know whether that trip you made to the auto repair shop actually fixed the rattle in your car. You know whether or not you actually did gain a pound from that banana split to which you treated yourself. You may even know the response from a friend whom you treated with kindness (or with anger) yesterday. You now know what happened yesterday and what the consequences of your actions and your thoughts are today, but yesterday you had free will, didn't you? Perhaps that's how God can know the future, because he is free to wander around outside the train. His knowledge does not affect our ability to make decisions – he loves us too much to turn us into obedient robots.

We've encountered some remarkable facts about time. Time depends on how fast you are traveling. Time had a beginning. Perhaps it is possible to be outside of time. Scientists have many other questions about time. Might there be other dimensions of time, as there are for space? In the simple train model I described, why does the train only seem to move forward? Why not backward too? There are many mysteries about time. Yet, one thing you and I already know about time, is that each of us is likely to run out of it during this earthly life. There is no time to waste in coming into relationship with God. I've heard people say, "You know, I think I'll get started back to church someday, after I get my life together." Well, church is not the place to go after you get your life together. It is the place you go *in order* to get your life together. If there is reconciliation that needs to be done in your life, do it now, with God and with the other people of your life. There is no time to waste.

Eric was a top scientist at the university, an accomplished experimental physicist. But Eric was also one of the most cynical and pessimistic people I've ever known. He had a really hard edge to him, and it seemed he never had a good thing to say about anybody. He was always expecting the worst to happen. As I got to know Eric better, I came to understand how life had wounded him deeply. His wife had left him years ago, and he was still shattered by that tragedy in his life, still devastated and deeply hurt, unable to forgive. Eric had few friends. Probably the closest thing to a friend that Eric had were a few casual work acquaintances like me. Eric rejected the idea of God, I suspect because of a deep cynicism that silently proclaimed, "How could anyone love me, because I'm so unlovable?" I remember loaning Eric a copy of C. S. Lewis' book, *Mere Christianity,* but I'm not sure he ever looked at it.

In any case, the book had no observable impact on Eric. It didn't seem like time was something Eric ever thought he might run out of.

One day Eric found out that he had terminal cancer. Eric actually laughed about it in a sneering sort of way, as if saying, "Doesn't it figure? I should have expected this." Eric saw himself as a loser: "This is the way my life has always been," he said to me one day, "so I'm not surprised at all." The doctors said Eric only had a year to live. And he did live only one year. Those few casual friends of Eric's like me began to ramp up our efforts in trying to talk to Eric about God: to tell him about God's love, about God's offer of forgiveness and eternal life. But it wasn't clear that we were having any impact at all. Every time I would talk with Eric about God, which I arranged to do about once a week, he would listen patiently but tight-lipped and unresponsive.

I remember the last night of Eric's life. We knew he was close to the end. Several of us organized an all-night vigil with him in the hospital, so that he would not be alone, each of us taking one hour at a time. I drew the four-to-five shift, and I'll never forget being there with Eric. He was very uncomfortable, sweaty, moaning, and constantly thirsty. But I could sense that Eric appreciated my being with him. As he drifted in and out of consciousness, I would pray. Four hours later, Eric, aged 43, was dead.

At his funeral, a pastor from the community stood up and shared how Eric, prompted by the urging of his friends, had been talking with him during the last months of his life. Eric had never let on to me or anyone else about this. The pastor read us a letter that Eric had written shortly before his death. He wrote that over the past few months, he had come to understand the love that God had for him. He wrote words to the effect, "I don't understand much about faith. I don't understand it any better than I did five years ago. God's existence and who he is and how he works are still a mystery to me, but I've come to know him personally." Then he wrote, "I've made a lot of mistakes, carried a lot of regrets with me, but these past two months, in spite of my illness, have been the happiest of my life."

8. What I Did for Love

Hunger for Knowledge, Hunger for Life

The famous astrophysicist Stephen Hawking wrote: "We find ourselves in a bewildering world. We want to make sense of what we see around us and to ask, 'What is the nature of the universe, what is our place in it and where did it and we come from? Why is it the way it is?'" [1] This is a question that transcends science and faith and speaks from the mind of every human.

This hunger to know why we are here and how we got here continues to inspire physics research. While some people of faith may believe that sufficient answers to these questions can be found in the testimony of Scripture, they follow the progress of science closely and delight in its discoveries. The psalmist tells us that God's creation is beautiful and worthy of study. There is nothing in ethical scientific inquiry to be feared or opposed by the person of faith. Yet, we have seen how an antagonistic relationship between science and religious faith developed in the 19th century. Some of that attitude persists today.

I remember a fellow student in college who delighted in the advances of modern biology, but his motives were suspect. He would share with me his excitement that any day now researchers would be able to produce life in the laboratory (that was thirty years ago). When this breakthrough occurs, he would gleefully proclaim, it would prove that God doesn't exist, because life could be produced without a divine creator. My friend's argument was very flawed, but I'm afraid some believers have bought into arguments such as this. So what if scientists are able to produce some simple form of life in the laboratory, after investing millions of research dollars and years of complex experiments under carefully controlled conditions? If that ever happened, wouldn't this just further confirm how unlikely it is that living organisms could develop by natural processes alone? Is faith that exists in fear of being disproved really faith at all?

When believers in God look at modern science, they find that scientific progress is not disproving religious faith at all (as was presupposed by some in 1900), but rather it is admitting more of a God possibility than ever, as an ever growing complexity of the universe is revealed. The tables may have been turned on atheists who rejoiced in the late 19th century about the demise of faith. One such example was an atheist philosopher named Ludwig Feuerbach, who argued that religious faith is just a mistaken expression of humankind's desires and longings, and that the resurrection story persists out of our fearful desire for immortality.[2]

Certainly, immortality is a longing of the human heart. People chase after immortality through a host of products and regimens that promise to keep them young, and we seek immortality through our kids and through our work. Overshadowing our longing for immortality is our fear of death and our knowledge of its inevitability. Woody Allen once said, "I don't want to achieve immortality through my work, I want to achieve it by not dying."[3] Yet, the believer in God trusts in the hope of eternal life, new life beginning now with spiritual rebirth, not because of fear but because of a promise, a promise from God.

In 1850 Ludwig Feuerbach wrote that people did not yet realize it, but natural science had "long before dissolved the Christian worldview in nitric acid."[4] Fortunately he was premature in his judgment.

Remarkably, there are important and surprising implications about life that have come from research into the Big Bang. As we turn our attention to these new findings about the universe, we must first look briefly at some *old* findings about the universe. There is a story here that we need to recall, the story of Galileo. In the life of this great scientist, we will see both positive and unproductive encounters between faith and science.

Science and the Church – the Story of Galileo

Before about 1600, the view of the universe that most people held and that the Church also held was the one you arrive at by simple observation, a good example of naïve reality. We would conclude that the earth is the center of the universe -- and in fact, the Church embraced this position, because it made humankind more important and demonstrated God's favor toward us. This is not biblical thinking, unless you refer to a couple of biblical references in a very literal way. However, this is the position that the Church took for at least a thousand years. Around the earth everything else revolved: the sun, the moon and the stars. Then in the late 1500s, two brilliant scientists, Copernicus and Johannes Kepler, began to overturn the old way of looking at the universe. From their astronomical studies, these pioneers concluded that indeed all the planets seemed to revolve around the sun. Yet their work was not seriously challenged by the Church (allowing them to be discussed only as hypothesis) until Galileo's fame brought attention to them.[5]

Of course today we know the truth about the relative significance of the earth in the universe. As Stephen Hawking points out, "The earth is a medium-sized planet orbiting around an average star in the outer suburbs of an ordinary spiral galaxy, which is itself only one of about a million million galaxies in the observable universe."[6]

Typical galaxies such as our own Milky Way may contain a hundred million stars. When you gaze into the night sky, all the stars that you see are in our Milky Way galaxy. The thin band of faint stars you can see on a clear night – that star gazers call the Milky Way -- is the edge of our spiral galaxy. The nearest galaxy to our Milky Way is Andromeda, which appears as only a faint star in our night sky. There are a million million galaxies in the observable universe. It's mind-boggling. That's what we know today about earth's place in the universe, and the story may be even more astounding, as some scientists propose the possible existence of an infinite number of universes! [7]

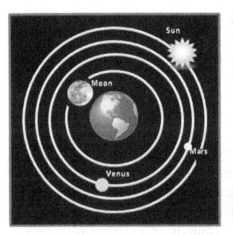 

Figure 2 – Before about 1600 the Church advocated a non-scientific and non-biblical view that the earth is the center of the universe, and all other planets and stars revolved around it (as shown on the left). Now we know that the earth is a small speck circling one average star in one average spiral galaxy, like M83, shown at the right (photographed by the European Southern Observatory's Wide Field Imager at La Silla, Chile). M83 is similar to our own Milky Way galaxy, which is roughly 700 billion times the sun's diameter and contains about a hundred million stars.

There may be 1,000,000,000,000,000,000,000 stars in the universe.

We've come a long way in understanding from the century before Galileo. Yet, the impact of Galileo was every bit as radical (and perhaps more significant) as detection of spiral galaxies and theories about parallel universes. Galileo lived from 1564 to 1642 in Italy, in the aftermath of the Protestant Reformation, a time when the Catholic Church was understandably more protective of doctrine. He was a remarkable man, probably one of the three greatest physicists, along with Newton and Einstein, who ever lived.

Consider just a short list of Galileo's remarkable accomplishments. Galileo invented the first astronomical telescope, completing it in just 24 hours![8] He invented the thermometer. He discovered the law of falling bodies and provided the foundation for Newton's later understanding of classical mechanics (we have mentioned his famous demonstration from the Leaning Tower of Pisa). After inventing the telescope, most people would have rested on their laurels, appeared on the Larry King Show, and considered a future in acting or politics. But Galileo was just warming up. He used his telescope to discover the craters on the moon. He discovered the rings of Saturn. He discovered sun spots. He discovered the moons of Jupiter, and he discovered and named a vast number of stars. It was his study of the tides which led him to the conclusion that the earth was not stationary, but revolves on its axis and orbits around the sun. [9] By this time Galileo, always outspoken, was already a celebrity. He was a frequent guest of Pope Urban VIII, and he was well known among the great college of Jesuit scientists, who may have seen Galileo as a competitor to their own research.

Today, everyone beyond the age of three knows that the earth revolves around the sun, but this is certainly not intuitive to our senses. Do you realize that the surface of the earth is spinning at 1,000 miles per hour and that the earth is moving around the sun at a speed of 67,000 miles per hour, and the whole solar system is moving an additional 500,000 mph through the Milky Way galaxy into regions of space our planet has never traversed before? And if you want to feel really uncomfortable, consider that scientists now say there are about a thousand asteroids in the projected path of the earth. Though the probability of a collision with an asteroid is unlikely, such an encounter could endanger all life on the planet. When science fiction movies show space ships traversing asteroid fields as they hurtle through space at mind-boggling speeds, remember that you are aboard such a ship at this moment! We're on a wild adventure! How can we ever consider life to be the same-old same-old again?

Galileo's assertion about the earth's movement challenged a Church doctrine which had no credible biblical basis. The Church's position was based on naïve reality (and rather far-fetched attempts to support it with Scripture) and also on our supposed importance to God: we must be the center of the universe! But Galileo was unafraid to take on a good challenge. He once said to his audience, "To demonstrate to my opponents the truth of my conclusions, I have been forced to prove them by a variety of experiments. Though to satisfy myself alone, I have never felt it necessary to make any experiments."[10] His self-confidence was great, and perhaps a person of lesser boldness would not have persevered in proclaiming this new scientific discovery.

Apparently Galileo was not much of a family man. He had three illegitimate children, which he dispensed with as soon as he could in his young life. His eldest daughter was sent off to a monastery as soon as she was a teenager, and it is said Galileo hoped that he would never see her again.[11] However, this daughter would later play an important and loving role in her father's life.

It is believed that professional jealousy of Galileo's celebrity status by his Jesuit colleagues may have played as great a role in his trial and conviction as a heretic as did his challenge to Church doctrine. Certainly, Galileo's own bluntness did not help, as he claimed that the research of his Jesuit colleagues was fiction, while he alone dealt with the facts.[12] Pope Urban VIII himself never did condemn Galileo; his sentence -- at the pleasure of the Cardinals, presumably for life -- was signed by seven of the ten cardinals. The Pope intervened and reduced Galileo's sentence to house arrest for an indeterminable amount of time.

Historian Will Durant articulates the Church's fear of Galileo's discovery:

> "Many theologians felt that the Copernican astronomy was so clearly incompatible with the Bible that if it prevailed, the Bible would lose authority and Christianity itself would suffer. What would happen to the fundamental Christian belief that God had chosen this earth as his human home? This earth, now to be shorn of its primacy and its dignity, to be set loose among planets so many times larger than itself, and among innumerable stars."[13]

In reacting as it did, the Church ignored the wise guidance of St. Augustine, written twelve centuries earlier (italics are my comments):

> "If they (*non-Christians*) find a Christian mistaken in a field which they themselves know well and hear him maintaining his foolish opinions about our books [*that is, the Bible*] then how are they going to believe those books in matters concerning the resurrection of the dead, the hope of eternal life, and the kingdom of heaven, when they think their pages are full of falsehoods on facts which they themselves have learnt from experience in the light of reason?"[14]

I wonder in what ways modern faith communities make the same kind of error made by the medieval Church in their confrontation with objective scientific discovery. Too often we see public forums pitting religious spokespersons against scientific spokespersons in discussions over contemporary scientific questions such as evolution, the age of the earth, or the existence of life on other planets – as if it is reasonable to assume that science and religious faith are naturally opposed to one another. Certainly scientific understanding may be wrong (or incomplete) at times or religious positions may not be well grounded – but a greater hazard of such science-versus-religion debates is the crystallization within the public mind that science and faith are naturally in opposition to one another. This is patently wrong. Both science and religion seek truth, though through different processes. Believers have little to fear from science; I have yet to encounter a confirmed scientific discovery that truly contradicts a thoughtful and prayerful reading of Scripture. Believers in God should be charitably promoting dialogue. Foolish reactions –based on shaky positions or poor theological scholarship – such as those which came from the Church in its challenge to Galileo are doomed to failure and (as Augustine reminds us) will damage a faithful proclamation of religious truth.

So what happened to Galileo? When the Pope commuted his prison sentence to house arrest, Galileo was confined to a Roman villa (which doesn't sound like such a grim fate). He was given considerable freedom during his imprisonment; he entertained famous guests (celebrities such as John Milton visited him), and he continued to study and even publish some of his works. As part of his sentence, Galileo was required to make confession of his alleged error, which he did, but tradition says (though it's not recorded anywhere) that as he was led out from the trial, he muttered audibly under his breath, referring to the earth, "Yet it moves." So Galileo may have gotten the last word, after all.

As part of Galileo's penance, he was required to recite seven penitential psalms every day for the next three years.[15] Although Galileo was a devout Catholic, this enforced piety no doubt rankled this proud man. It was Galileo's daughter, the one Galileo had sent off to a convent in her teenage years, who came to her father's aid. In the convent, Galileo's daughter became a woman of devout faith and great character. After her father's house arrest, she came and lived with him and stayed with him the rest of his life. She cared for him and nurtured him. And she took on the job every day of saying those seven penitential psalms for him.[16] Each day she read the psalms, out loud, to her father. One wonders what softening impact this lovely woman must have had upon the heart of a proud and wounded man.

The error of the Church's position on the motion of the earth was in fearing that the concept of an earth that is not the center of everything would diminish the importance of humankind. Of course the truth is much more severe than even Galileo could imagine: we're on an insignificant little planet on the outskirts of interstellar nowhere, in the boondocks of the universe. But why should we have ever expected that anything different was true in the first place? What biblical assertion about humankind would lead anyone to suspect that earth must be the center of the universe? That we are so important, so deserving of such favor? The biblical understanding of humankind is that out of our own power alone we are finite and doomed for death. There is nothing that we have done, there is nothing that we can do, to command or deserve God's love or favor, absolutely nothing. God makes it clear that without him we can do nothing. His favor towards humankind is an unmerited gift, which we call grace, and it has nothing at all to do with our being the center of anything other than the apple of his eye.

Galileo's discovery was the most important development in understanding the universe until the discovery of the Big Bang in 1929. As we dig further into understanding the Big Bang, we will see evidence of religious people once again making the same kind of mistake they made with Galileo.

Why Is There Something Instead of Nothing?

Since Hubble's great discovery of the expanding universe, much scientific research has been devoted to confirming and understanding the Big Bang. Though incomplete, data are sufficient to test theoretical models in describing the universe all the way back to within fractions of a second after its beginning. We know the approximate size of the universe, its expansion rate, and the abundance of stars and elements. We know the basic laws of physics, and we have some strong physics theories to apply to the problem (quantum mechanics and general relativity). However, when all of our physics tools were brought to bear upon the problem of analyzing the Big Bang, the scientific world was in for several big surprises, the impact of which still have us reeling today. Among the startling surprises, we have learned that our premiere physics theories are incomplete, and we have learned that we cannot account for all the matter that calculations say must be present if the universe. We'll take this up in Chapter 9.

One of the most provocative findings from Big Bang research, unveiled in the 1970s, is the discovery of the so-called anthropic principle, which comes from the Greek word for *human*. The anthropic principle is a collection of scientific data that makes the startling implication: the universe appears to be finely tuned in just such a delicate way as to make possible the existence of life on at least one planet.

One of the pieces of data we can use in testing any theory of the Big Bang is the known existence of a planet with carbon-based life, our earth. Any correct theory obviously must allow for the production of what we know as earth and life as we know it. But in order to allow for a planet like earth to be formed, scientists have found that many of the basic parameters of nature and laws of physics had to be very finely tuned. That is, there are dozens of properties -- from nuclear properties to chemical and atomic properties of matter -- that must have just the right values.[17] If these properties are adjusted just a small bit, a planet like earth could never have been formed from the Big Bang.

Stephen Hawking, an agnostic, remarkably concludes,

"This means that the initial state of the universe must have been very carefully chosen indeed if the hot big bang model is correct back to the beginning of time. It would be very difficult to explain why the universe should have begun in this way except as an act of a god who intended to create beings like us."[18]

I will mention just a few of the many finely tuned properties to give you a flavor of the situation.[17,19] For carbon – the elemental building block of life – to have initially been created inside stars, the strength of the *nuclear strong force* could not vary by more than 1 percent from its known value. If the *proton-neutron mass difference* (about one part in a thousand) had not been almost exactly twice the electron's mass, then all neutrons would have decayed into protons or else all protons would have changed irreversibly into neutrons. Either way, there would be no stable atoms upon which all of biology and chemistry are based. If the *electromagnetic force* were only very slightly different, then all stars would either be much colder or much hotter, making the conditions for life impossible. Do you know that if the water molecule behaved like most other molecules – that is, it's density increased upon freezing -- then ice would be heavier than liquid water, and lakes and oceans would freeze from the bottom up. If this were true, the whole earth would eventually be buried under ice. It's not that way. There are many more amazing examples of fine tuning, involving the force of gravity, the way carbon atoms interact with sunlight, the number of stars in the universe, and so on. Brian Greene, a theoretical physicist at Columbia University, relates all these finely tuned properties to the elementary particles, which "are entwined with what many view as the deepest question in all science: *Why do the elementary particles have just the right properties to allow nuclear processes to happen, stars to light up, planets to form around stars, and on at least one planet, life to exist?*"[20]

Critics of the anthropic principle, admittedly struggling to find real chinks in its armor, have proposed a watered-down version called the Weak Anthropic Principle. Advocates of this view say that if the universe were not finely-tuned, then humans would not be here to observe it. Thus, fine tuning requires no real explanation. But, as Stephen Meyer, a science historian, points out, "Though we should not be surprised to find ourselves living in a universe suited for life (by definition), we ought to be surprised to learn the conditions necessary for life are so vastly improbable."[21] And that needs an explanation.

To help us understand the situation, philosopher John Leslie presents the following scary story.[22] Imagine you were convicted of some capital crime and were sentenced to die by firing squad. God forbid that should happen to you! But let's imagine that you're hauled out to be shot by the firing squad, and there are a hundred expert marksmen with high-powered, loaded rifles aimed right at you. The captain of the guard gives the command, and the marksmen fire. A hundred expert marksmen. And they all miss. Now do you walk away from that and say 'Phew, I guess I got lucky today,' or do you say 'There must be some other explanation for this!'? Could all those one hundred skilled marksmen simultaneously be having a bad hair day and accidentally miss you? Or was there an intentionality in sparing you? In the same way, the findings of modern science that our being here is very strange and unlikely require an explanation. We cannot say, "Phew, I guess I just got lucky."

Undoubtedly, we will learn that some of the dozens of finely-tuned properties that have been reported are incorrect or can be readily explained. But can they all be wrong? Some have attempted explanations for the anthropic principle that are entirely natural and do not imply a creative force,[23] and such work will continue, but there appears to be a near consensus among scientists at this time of amazement and bewilderment about the implications of the anthropic principle.

Particle physicist Gordon Kane concludes that there are only two possible explanations for the amazing fine tuning we observe in our universe.[23] One is that a fine-tuner must have prepared the Big Bang in just this special life-accommodating way. The only other possibility offered by scientists today is that there may be an infinite number of universes (or that our universe is infinitely cyclic), and we just happen to be in one of the very rare universes (or rare cycles of one universe) that allow life. There presently is absolutely no credible evidence of other universes, but neither are there any reasons (even including biblical) why there couldn't be. The current view of most scientists is that the parallel universe hypothesis is too speculative.

Even if our universe is one of many, or is cyclic, a challenging question remains, and that is, why is there even a universe at all as opposed to just the possibility of a universe? The great mathematician Leibniz once pondered, "Why is there something instead of nothing?"[24] Or as astrophysicist Stephen Hawking asks: "What is it that breathes fire into the equations and makes a universe for them to describe?" The usual approach of science of constructing a mathematical model cannot answer the question of why there should be a universe for the model to describe. Why does the universe go to all the bother of existing?"[25]

John Polkinghorne adds that even in the absence of a universe, where did the laws of physics come from that would make it even possible.[26] A few years back, the following tee shirt was popular among physics students: it read, "And God said," followed by the electromagnetic equations of Maxwell (which describe all radiation), then "and there was light." A theologically significant tee shirt!

Somehow a universe has developed from the Big Bang with just the right conditions to produce and sustain carbon-based life on at least one planet. The vast majority of the universe is hot, ionized gas -- very high temperature matter that's inhospitable to any kind of life as we know it. And yet here we are on this amazing planet teeming with the breath of life in sea gulls, butterflies and human beings; soil that grows crabgrass, corn, and redwood trees; and water spilling into mountain brooks and pounding upon rugged seashores. It's an amazing thing. And the possibility that something like this could randomly have happened is starting to look as probable as having the winning Power Ball ticket ten times in a row. If you won all those Power Ball lotteries, people would probably be suspicious that there was a conspiracy, wouldn't they? And it would probably be true; somebody set the whole thing up. So it seems more and more like the universe was set up in a finely-tuned way from the beginning.

This is not just the wishful thinking of religious writers. Here are the conclusions of two of the distinguished scientists of our era.

Freeman Dyson is one of the preeminent theoretical physicists of our time, famous for his work in quantum field theory, solid-state physics, and nuclear engineering. He says of all this, "The more I examine the universe and the details of its architecture, the more evidence I find that the universe in some sense must have known we were coming." [27]

Owen Gingerich is Professor of Astronomy and of the History of Science, Emeritus, in the Department of Astronomy at the Harvard-Smithsonian Center for Astrophysics. He writes, "To me, belief in a final cause, a Creator-God, gives coherent understanding of why the universe seems so congenially designed for the existence of intelligent, self-reflective life. It would take only small changes in numerous physical constants to render the universe uninhabitable."[28]

Again, it is important to acknowledge that our scientific understanding of the Big Bang is still in relative infancy. There is much that is still not understood or agreed upon. There is much that will be learned in the decades ahead, and these findings may cause us to rethink the whole idea of the anthropic principle. There are many important questions in our current scientific understanding of the universe.[29] Why does the expansion of the universe seem to speeding up, rather than slowing down? What caused the apparent very rapid expansion of the early universe during the first fraction of a second (the so-called inflationary stage) of the Big Bang? What comprises the 'dark matter' that must be present in great abundance in the universe? How do we theoretically explain gravity? And so on.

Belief in God comes from faith and not science. I concur with Cardinal John Henry Newman, who wrote: "I believe in intelligent design because I believe in a designer; I do not believe in a designer because I see evidence of design." [30] Yet it is important to know whether the basic principles and documents of faith in God are in conflict with what we are learning from science. I believe that they are not. New findings about the origin of our universe are tantalizing and encouraging, and perhaps this should not be surprising to those with faith in God. The Bible says, "As it is written, what no eye has seen, nor ear heard, nor human heart conceived, what God has prepared for those who love him."[31] Perhaps what God has prepared for us is beyond what we can grasp – what he has prepared in creation, what he has prepared in our life, what he is preparing now for our future. As we will see, however, while we may not be able to grasp the workings of God's creation, we can grasp his love.

Another View: Faith is a Delusion

Some scientists – like others in our culture -- are adamantly opposed to any suggestion that God may exist. Perhaps the best known among modern scientist atheists is Richard Dawkins, the renowned evolutionary biologist from Oxford University. His best-selling book *The God Delusion* is a wide-ranging denouncement of religion. He is upfront about his goal for the book: "If this book works as I intend, religious readers who open it will be atheists when they put it down. What presumptuous optimism! Of course, dyed-in-the-wool faith-heads are immune to argument, their resistance built up over years of childhood indoctrination ..." [32]

The conclusion for the first half of *The God Delusion* is that "God almost certainly does not exist."[33] Dawkins has two primary arguments for the non-existence of God. Briefly, the first is that Darwin's theory explains almost everything about the universe, not requiring the necessity of invoking a creative source.[34] Yet, Dawkins can offer no alternative explanation for the remarkable findings that comprise the anthropic principle other than referring to them as an "initial stroke of luck" in the origin of the universe.[35] While he admits that God is "not technically disprovable,"[36] his second primary argument against God being responsible for a complex creation is that this God would have to be a very complex entity, which he deems as improbable.[37] He concludes this argument with "the familiar question 'Who made God?', which most thinking people discover for themselves. A designer God cannot be used to explain organized complexity because any God capable of designing anything would have to be complex enough to demand the same kind of explanation in his own right." [38]

To my mind, the very kind of God that Dawkins claims is so improbable is exactly the kind of God who in fact exists. Yes, God must be very complex – his ways are higher than our ways -- and this has always been the understanding of faithful people. This God of the Judeo-Christian faith traditions is a God who was not created at all nor was the result of an evolutionary process, but who was there at the beginning of all things, and created everything that is from nothing. Is this an improbable God? Absolutely! But as new findings such as the anthropic principle are indicating, the existence of life on a planet such as ours, or even the existence of such a life-friendly planet is extremely improbable. As Alister McGrath, Professor of Historical Theology at Oxford University and molecular biophysicist, states, "... improbability does not, and never has, entailed nonexistence. We may be highly improbable – *yet we are here*. The question then is not whether God is *probable*, but whether God is *actual*." [39]

Dawkins' ideas about God have generated much controversy and much criticism from fellow scientists for falling short of the scientific objectivity that has characterized so much of his fine genetics research (and that is my take on *The God Delusion,* as well). Alister McGrath pulls no punches in referring to Dawkins' arguments for God's nonexistence as "half-baked nonsense."[40] and finds it curious that "there is surprisingly little scientific analysis in *The God Delusion.*"[41] Similar criticism has come from Francis Collins, one of the world's leading geneticists and Director of the National Institutes of Health. In his former work as head of the National Human Genome Project, Collins and his team pioneered genetic research that has helped us move toward cures for diseases such as cystic fibrosis and Huntington's Disease. He writes about *The God Delusion,* "Dawkins is a master of setting up a straw man, and then dismantling it with great relish. In fact, it is hard to escape the conclusion that such repeated mischaracterizations of faith betray a vitriolic personal agenda, rather than a reliance on the rational arguments that Dawkins so cherishes in the scientific realm."[42] It is interesting that both McGrath and Collins are one-time atheists who became believers in God as adults.

Dawkins' arguments for the nonexistence of God, using ideas from Darwin's theory, force people to take sides; if you accept the findings of evolutionary biology, you cannot believe in a creator God, and vice versa. This is tragic. I recall a man, who visited our church to hear one of my forums on science, telling me, "Oh, I could never believe in God, because I believe in evolution," as if somehow they are mutually exclusive ideas. Much new work is showing that there is a compatibility between the findings of evolutionary biology and belief in a creator God and that the polarization that has characterized so much of the science and religion discourse is unnecessary.[43]

If we are truly interested in pursuing truth, we are best served by the avenues presented to us by both science and religion, and I believe we will find them not to be in conflict. Renowned physicist Freeman Dyson reminds us, "Science and religion are two windows that people look through, trying to understand the big universe outside, trying to understand why we are here. The two windows give different views, but they look out at the same universe. Both views are one-sided, neither is complete. Both leave out essential features of the real world. And both are worthy of respect."[44]

Opposition to the idea of God's existence is certainly intellectually respectable (though I believe in error), and there are many atheists whose integrity and thoughtful commitment to pursuit of the truth is very high. As Dawkins concedes, and as most thoughtful believers will concur, the existence of God can probably not be proved or disproved by science alone, and this will likely fuel spirited dialogue for a long time. There are some more extreme, even hostile, voices from the scientific community, however. Here is how prominent chemist Peter Atkins thinks about religion, a rather extreme view even among atheists:

> "The religious will increasingly have no excuse for continued belief in the existence of God but will nevertheless cling to it. Indeed, as science exposes the ultimate bleakness of the universe -- a bleakness I find enthralling -- it is likely that humanity will cling increasingly to the false hope provided by religion ... They want comforting thoughts, not truth."[45]

Atkins has also said that "faith is one of the world's great evils, comparable to the smallpox virus but harder to eradicate."[46]

When such opposition becomes extreme, sources other than intellectual integrity may be at work. Francis Collins, a leader in articulating the relationship between science and faith, states that his own faith grew primarily from the testimony of the Gospels. He writes, "The evidence for the authenticity of the four gospels turns out to be quite strong." [47]

He claims that his own change from being an atheist to a person of faith came from grasping the truth of the resurrection, but that for a long time "my desire to draw close to God was blocked by my own pride and sinfulness, which in turn was an inevitable consequence of my selfish desire to be in control." [48]

Yes, admission of the existence of God has great implications for one's life. As John Polkinghorne says, "I believe in quarks, but the acknowledgement of their existence does not touch or threaten me in my own being. It is very different with a belief in God, which has consequences for all that I do and hope for."[49]

Few scientists share the strong views of Peter Atkins or Richard Dawkins, and many who profess no belief in God are struck by the evidence for a purposeful creator of the universe. Physicist Paul Davies, an agnostic, writes,

> "I cannot believe that our existence in this universe is a mere quirk of fate, an accident of history, an incidental blip in the great cosmic drama. The existence of mind in some organism on some planet in the universe is surely a fact of fundamental significance. This can be no minor product of mindless, purposeless forces. We are truly meant to be here."[50]

I see it as compelling (and beautiful) to imagine a God-given intention for the creation of the universe. To help us appreciate the image of a loving creator, preparing an earthly home for us, imagine an expectant mother preparing a room before her baby is born. New frilly curtains go up, a new crib is made ready, with little hanging baby toys for the child's learning and amusement, new clothes bought and neatly stored in the room -- everything is just right. If you walked into that room and looked around before that baby is born, you'd know exactly what's going to happen! That mom is preparing for the birth of a child, isn't she? And you can also imagine the joyous smiles on the future momma's face as she prepares the room for her baby. Is that what God has done in preparing this whole universe - to set up a special place for his children, right from the beginning? He prepared it with us in mind. God says in Scripture, "For surely I know the plans I have for you, plans for your welfare and not for harm, to give you a future of hope."[51] And God's act of creation wasn't just a momentary thing; it goes on in our lives each day, as he continues his creation in us. The Bible says, "Be glad for what God is planning for you. Be patient in trouble and always be prayerful."[52] If God has prepared this elaborate universe and this amazing earth, where we could experience life, do you think he put us here just to twist slowly in the wind? The Bible says, "For it is the God who said, 'Let light shine out of darkness,' who has shone in our hearts to give the light of the knowledge of the glory of God in the face of Jesus Christ."[53]

Yet, for some, this idea of a God of outrageous love and stop-at-nothing determination to nurture and save his creation is hard to grasp. Stephen Hawking shares his reservations: "The strong anthropic principle would claim that this whole vast construction exists simply for our sake. This is hard to believe."[54] While our religious traditions offer no view as to whether or not we are alone in the universe, neither do they offer any reason why God would not create a vast universe just for our sake. Christians, for example, believe that God has done much more for the world than create a universe of stars by sending his only son to die for us. The death of Christ came at much greater cost to God than his construction costs for building a universe even as large and complex as ours. And, who is to say what the significance of space and time is to God? The Bible says, "Do not ignore this one fact, beloved, that with the Lord one day is like a thousand years and a thousand years are like one day."[55] Do the dimensions of space and time, as we measure them, mean that much to God?

The Bible, as mentioned earlier, is not to be viewed as a textbook on science. It devotes only a short section of one book to the creation of the universe and then the whole remainder of the Bible to his relationship with humankind. To God, the creation of the universe may not be that big of a topic. Unbelievably, we humans seem to be what's most important to God. And yet, Stephen Hawking's incredulity is absolutely understandable. It's hard to imagine God doing this. Only a God of outrageous love and extravagance would do such a thing!

Good News and Bad News

Here is the ultimate good news and bad news story. The good news is that we are loved outrageously by God, out of all proportion, incredibly, ridiculously; it makes no sense at all. And in fact, we ourselves would have never lavished such love on a straying people like us, but that's what God apparently has done. As Archbishop Desmond Tutu has said with a twinkle in his eye, "This God has appallingly low standards!"[56] That's the good news.

The bad news is summed up in a story about my friend, Alan. Alan was and is a brilliant and articulate theoretical physicist, a gentle and kind person. I always enjoyed Alan's company. I knew Alan when I was doing research in California, and I always admired his extraordinary research skills. Alan had been a member of the research team for a long time, but he was now dealing with professional burn-out. Though he was still a very productive member of the team, Alan had concluded that maybe it was time for some kind of a change, but he didn't know what that might be.

On a number of occasions I had chatted briefly with Alan about faith, but he was absolutely convinced that this whole idea of God made no sense at all. I remember one day going to lunch with Alan and thinking, well, this is the time that

I need to talk to him about faith in God. Alan knew I was a Christian, and out of his kindness he always tolerated my religious talk, even though it made no sense to him. So this was my chance: I told him about my faith. But Alan would hear nothing of it. He had rational bulletproof arguments for everything I would bring up. He was more articulate than I and he knew more about science than I and he could out-argue me on every point I would try to make. Talk about shooting free throws with Kobe Bryant! I was taking a beating; end of discussion, no point continuing. Alan was not going to hear anything about it. I was discouraged.

And so for awhile we ate our lunches in silence. Then Alan started talking about his life, and he began telling me about how his marriage was falling apart. In fact, some weeks went by when he and his wife barely spoke to one another, and he told me how difficult that had been. He told me about his grown daughter who never called or came to see him any more, and he was concerned about that relationship. Alan was unsure about his future. What should he do? Where did he go from here? He was looking ahead to his older years and all he could see was a fog. As Alan talked, I realized that all of his objections to God were not based ultimately on any kind of scientific argument. Rather, they were based on the fact that he could not grasp that God loved him. I saw before me a man who had not been loved enough in his life; he just couldn't accept that God could love him, because nobody else had.

There he was, a man lonely, longing for a relationship. And here was this God, seeking him, offering a relationship that could change his life. Alan was talking to me about knowledge, I was talking to him about faith, but the real subject of our discussion should have been love. The Bible says: "... if I have prophetic powers, and understand all mysteries and all knowledge, and if I have all faith, so as to remove mountains, but do not have love, I am nothing."[57]

So the good news is that we are deeply loved, but the bad news is that Alan and Stephen Hawking and many of us don't live as if we really know it.

For a moment, let's listen to what Scripture has to say about love, God's love for us, and our love for him and each other. As you reflect on these passages, think about a creative and nurturing God who is alive today, who loves us more than we can grasp, who is longing for a relationship with us, and who waits for our response.

From the Book of Genesis: "And God said, let us make humankind in our image, according to our likeness, and let them have dominion over the fish of the sea and over the birds of the air and over the cattle, and over all the wild animals of the earth, and over every creeping thing that creeps upon the earth. So God created humankind in his image; in the image of God he created them, male and female he created them. God blessed them and God said to them, 'Be fruitful and multiply, and fill the earth and subdue it, and have dominion over the fish of the sea and over the birds of the air and over every living thing that moves upon the earth.' God said, 'See, I have given you every plant yielding seed that is upon the face of all the earth, and every tree with seed in its fruit, you shall have them for food, and every beast of the earth and every bird of the air and to everything that creeps on the earth, everything that has the breath of life, I have given every green plant for food.' And it was so. God saw everything that he had made and indeed it was very good."[58]

From the Gospel of Mark: "You shall love the Lord your God with all your heart, and with all your soul, and with all your mind, and with all your strength."[59]

From the Gospel of John: "For God so loved the world that he gave his only Son, so that everyone who believes in him may not perish but have eternal life."[60]

From Isaiah: "Surely he has borne our infirmities and carried our diseases; yet we accounted him stricken, struck down by God, and afflicted. But he was wounded for our transgressions, crushed for our iniquities; upon him was the punishment that made us whole, and by his bruises we are healed."[61]

From the First Letter of John: "We love because He first loved us."[62]

From John's Gospel: "Jesus said, 'I give you a new commandment, that you love one another. Just as I have loved you, you also should love one another. By this everyone will know that you are my disciples, if you have love one for another.'"[63]

From the Book of Lamentations: "The steadfast love of the Lord never ceases, his mercies never come to an end; they are new every morning."[64]

From the First Letter of John: "God is love."[65]

From First Corinthians: "(Of all the spiritual gifts), the greatest are faith, hope and love. But the greatest of these is love.[66]

From John's Gospel: "Jesus said to Peter, 'Peter, do you love me?'"[67]

From the Letter to the Romans: "For I am sure that neither death, nor life, nor angels, nor principalities, nor things present, nor things to come, nor powers, nor height, nor depth, nor anything else in all creation, will be able to separate us from the love of God in Christ Jesus our Lord."[68]

I remember having breakfast in a local coffee shop one morning. As I sipped my coffee, waiting for my omelet to arrive, I noticed a smartly-dressed woman walk into the restaurant. She was wearing a well-tailored business suit and had a cell phone at her ear, talking hurriedly and seriously, closing a deal or making an important decision. I recognized her as a program manager for research, an accomplished scientist. With her day-timer tucked under her arm, she made her way through the tables to join the person she was meeting. No doubt an important meeting was about to transpire. She came to a table near where I was sitting and sat down next to a young woman who had a few-month-old baby in a baby seat next to her. The program manager piled her daytimer and cell phone onto an empty chair, then for a moment she just stared at that cute baby. Then the capable scientist leaned over, with a big smiling goofy look on her face, and went something like, "Oh, goo goo, look at da widdle baby, coochie coo." In the presence of a little child, all her competent professionalism was swept aside by overwhelming love – to the point where she didn't care about anything – even her dignity – didn't care about anything except this beautiful child.

Perhaps that's the way God feels about us. The Competent One set the stars in motion, invented gravity and quantum mechanics, created the elements, and made the plants and animals: tadpoles, mountain goats and redwood trees – but when God looks at us, he is so overcome by love that he just wants to cuddle us and talk baby talk.

9. Small Talk: the Weird World of Quantum Mechanics and Strings

Strange Behavior

Our discussion about the universe, as understood at the end of the twentieth century, must include a mention of the second great workhorse physics theory to be developed in that century: quantum mechanics. Quantum mechanics takes us from the world of the very large objects like stars, down to things the size of atoms or smaller. The discovery of quantum mechanics came at a time when, as we have discussed earlier, there was great confidence that almost all physics had been discovered. The laws of motion and mechanics that Isaac Newton had developed, the mathematical tools and the theories of electrodynamics that James Clerk Maxwell and Michael Faraday had developed in the 1800s, made it look like everything about our physical world was understood, except for a few little minor details that you might easily sweep under the scientific rug. (How many times in our own lives have we swept minor details under the rug and they have come back to haunt us later on, and we realized they weren't so minor after all?)

Fortunately, a few physicists like Max Planck, Erwin Schroedinger, and Werner Heisenberg were not willing to ignore the minor details. And their unraveling 'minor details' led to the surprising new development of quantum mechanics, which revolutionized our understanding of physics in the 20th century. Quantum mechanics is a very complicated subject. I was successful in several years of university coursework in quantum mechanics. Throughout my career as a physicist, I applied the principles of quantum mechanics to my research. I was competent at the required mathematical manipulations, yet I never could fully understand quantum mechanics at an intuitive level. And that's a hard pill for a physicist to swallow, because you want to understand it intuitively, you want it to jell in your mind and make sense. But very few people have had that experience.

The famed Nobel Laureate, Richard Feynman, who made great contributions to quantum mechanics (development of a field called quantum electrodynamics), was one of the great teachers and engaging speakers of the twentieth century. He said of quantum mechanics:

> "There was a time when the newspaper said that there were only twelve people in the world who understood the theory of relativity. I do not believe that there ever was such a time. There might have been a time when only one man did, because he was the only guy who caught on, before he wrote his paper. But after people read the paper, a lot of people understood the theory of relativity. On the other hand, I think I can safely say that nobody understands quantum mechanics."[1]

Quantum mechanics tells us that very small objects behave in ways surprisingly different from what Isaac Newton's laws of motion would predict. We'll look at just two important but strange features of quantum mechanics in this short survey. The first feature is called the quantization of energy, which applies to objects the size of atoms or smaller, an electron in an atom, for example. The classical physics of Newton says that a particle – let's say a billiard ball -- can move at any speed and thus have any kinetic energy, depending on the force that accelerates it. But quantum mechanics says that for very small objects, like an electron inside an atom, this is not the case at all. Rather, there are only certain allowed values of energy (called energy levels) that an electron inside an atom (a subatomic billiard ball, you might say) can have.

Imagine you had a quantum-mechanical car. A very microscopic car, it might have a speedometer that would only go 10 or 20 or 30 or 40 miles per hour and nothing in between. And as you stepped on the gas pedal, it would stay at the present speed until enough energy had been supplied to allow the car to jump to the next speed. (Hmm, I remember actually having an old junker car like that in college.) That would be a very strange thing. So the energy that a very tiny object can have only exists in finite chunks, called quanta. This is very strange -- it's totally non-intuitive -- but it's exactly the way the building-block particles inside an atom behave, and it's the law that controls how microcircuits in computers, lasers, and the atoms in all matter work.

A second feature of quantum mechanics is even more startling and hard to grasp. Quantum mechanics says that there are basic uncertainties in the way things behave. You may have heard of the Heisenberg Uncertainty Principle that's at the heart of quantum mechanics. Quantum mechanics says that there is a fundamental limit to how well certain properties of an object can be defined, and effect of this limit is especially important for small objects like atoms. If you know with high accuracy the location of a particle, for instance, there will be a large uncertainty in knowing its speed, and vice versa. This is not saying that there is just a lack of precision in how we measure small things (although quantum mechanics has a bearing on that too). Rather, the laws of quantum mechanics state that certain fundamental properties (like the location of the particle) have inherent uncertainties and can only be described by probabilities. If you play a game of pool with normal-sized billiard balls, a ball will move in the same definite and predictable way every time, if you hit it the same way each time. Quantum mechanics says that if there's an interaction between some very microscopic (atomic-sized) billiard balls, there are only probabilities about what may happen. There's inherent uncertainty in the outcome. As Brian Greene points out, "The universe, according to quantum mechanics, is *not* etched into the present; the universe, according to quantum mechanics, participates in a game of chance ... plainly speaking, this is weird."[2]

Even Albert Einstein never fully bought into all the implications of quantum mechanics. Regarding the probabilistic aspects of quantum mechanics, he once wrote to Werner Heisenberg, who had discovered the principles of uncertainty required by quantum mechanics, in an oft-quoted line, "God does not play dice with the universe." It is said that Heisenberg responded, "Even the great Einstein does not tell God what to do!"

The discovery of the probabilistic nature of matter caused many scientists, and no small number of theologians, problems. You mean to say there's uncertainty in the universe? For the physicist grounded in Newtonian mechanics, this idea is incredible. For some believers in God, the suggestion that God has not prescribed a definite outcome to an event is frightening.* Let's illustrate this probabilistic picture of reality with a very simple example. Let's imagine the simplest of all atoms, the hydrogen atom. There is one tiny particle called an electron orbiting around a nucleus, which for hydrogen is a single proton. In classical mechanics we envision this atom like a tiny solar system, with the electron (like a planet) orbiting around the proton (like a sun). But this is not a realistic picture at all. Because the electron is so tiny and has such a high speed, quantum mechanics predicts that there is a large inherent uncertainty in its location at a given moment. Its location is represented no longer as a specific particle but as a smear, or electron cloud, which represents the

---

*Of course, a conviction of many religious people is that God has given us free will, which means that our actions already introduce uncertainly into the outcome of events.

reality that the electron's position is only given by a probability of finding it in a given location. If you are going to study atoms and the particles that comprise them, you can only do it correctly with quantum mechanics.

Our common sense tells us that we could place a marble inside of a sealed coffee can and it would stay inside, no matter how you shake it, unless someone took the lid off. You could shake the can, turn it upside down, do whatever you want, but the marble would remain inside the coffee can. Quantum mechanics says that there is some inherent uncertainty in the position of the marble, and that its position can only be described by a probability. Therefore, at any moment the marble may actually appear outside the coffee can, without your having taken the lid off! Of course, the probability of this happening is large only for atom-sized objects, and can in fact be of great significance to our lives. The phenomenon of quantum tunneling, instrumental in how many modern electronic devices work, is a direct result of this probabilistic nature of small objects. Because the probability of the location of a small object is smeared out over space, there is a finite chance that a particle, say an electron, can be found outside – or tunnel through – an energy barrier that confines it. The computer chips inside the machine on which I am writing this sentence depends on this principle for operation! Yet, there is still a very small, yet finite, uncertainty even for larger objects like marbles. However, the probability is so small that you and I should not invest any time watching for this to happen! Nonetheless, remember quantum mechanics the next time you go to the zoo, and you're standing there at the lion's cage. From one second to the next there's a finite probability that the lion could be outside the cage! It's actually true. So be careful. (Of course, I'm kidding about your need to worry about the lion. Yet, I am still trying to understand the mysterious disappearance of socks from my dresser drawer and the equally mysterious appearance of new coat hangers in my closet. Hmm.)

Sweating the Small Stuff

How does quantum mechanics affect our understanding of God?

On the one hand, you might say that quantum mechanics only deals with very small things, so maybe it's not very important to me. Don't sweat the small stuff! I mean, seriously, how can this be important to my life? Isn't quantum mechanics just a small detail? You might ask, what does quantum mechanics have to do with the taste of strawberries, the price of gas at the pump, the video game on my iPad, or the copper wires in my wall? Well, just about everything! Quantum mechanics is at the heart of how all matter behaves – it is at the root of how molecules bond, how atoms move, how matter holds together. It is at the very heart of our physical reality. It is much more than a small detail! You cannot ignore quantum mechanics.

But on the other hand, you might make too much of it. You could say, "Doesn't the probabilistic nature of quantum mechanics mean that the outcomes of all atomic scale events are uncertain and therefore the outcome of large scale events must be similarly uncertain and therefore the destiny of the universe is uncertain? Where is there any place for a creative God in a universe like that?" It is important for us to realize that while quantum mechanics shows that there is a probabilistic nature to reality, quantum mechanics is governed by precise, solvable equations that have specific solutions. While there is a limit to the precision of a quantum measurement, that uncertainty is known. While the position of a quantum particle is described by a probability, that probability is known and can be calculated in a straightforward (although often mathematically difficult) manner. And these calculated probabilities lead to specific and reproducible results for the large scale systems and events we observe around us.

For me, pondering the amazing world of quantum mechanics only brings awe for an amazing universe. For those who see the universe as the purposeful act of God, quantum mechanics cautions us to avoid putting God in a box, requiring God to conform to our naïve sense of reality. If anything, quantum mechanics teaches us that God is God, and we're not. We should always give thanks for God's incredible creation and thank him that he has given us minds to study the astounding reality he has set before us. Thank God for inventing quantum mechanics as well as allowing us to discover it.

Shock, fear and denial in response to new scientific discoveries (assuming they are true) are not a truly faithful attitude. The psalmist writes, "Great are the works of the Lord, studied by all who delight in them."[3] Believers are not to be like the fearful church of Galileo's day, when parishioners were forbidden to peer through Galileo's newly developed telescope. Creation is to be studied and handled and grasped and pursued.

Quantum Philosophy?

As we have seen, quantum mechanics teaches us to be careful about trusting our naïve reality. Often our culture tells us to trust our 'common sense,' 'get our heads out of the clouds,' 'keep our feet on the ground.' Quantum mechanics causes us not to trust that common sense by showing us that for very small systems like atoms, reality is not at all the way we perceive it in our macroscopic world. There is a limit to how well we can define properties of a particle like its location and its speed. Quantum mechanics tells us that it is impossible to measure the properties of a particle without altering the state of that particle. It shows us how particles can be correlated and connected to one another, even over great distances. It explains how the outcome of processes are governed, not by precise destinies, but only by probabilities. Quantum mechanics teaches us that we must be grounded in a reality that is truly real, and not just the projection of our limited senses.

One can make the opposite error too in anticipating a "quantum" solution to all matters, so much that it might be a foundation for philosophy. For example, some have attempted to cite the uncertainty principle in support of postmodern arguments against absolute truth.[4] Though I will say a few words here, the quantum mechanical implications for philosophy is a complicated topic and beyond the scope of our discussion, but it has been well reviewed in several good discussions.[5,6]

It is trendy for gurus of various sorts to brandish quantum mechanical terms, as if to give credibility to their philosophical speculations. We may hear vague terms like "everything is energy" or "there can be no such thing as certainty" or "everything is connected," terms designed to give a philosophical conjecture some measure of scientific respectability. While there is much we do not yet grasp about the implications of quantum mechanics, I think one should be suspicious of such language, remembering that quantum mechanics applies in a significant way only to very small particles, and even there it applies in well-defined, albeit very weird, ways. We would do well to heed the caution of John Polkinghorne: Remember that "your average quantum mechanic is about as philosophically minded as your average garage mechanic."[7]

Dark Cloud Looming – the Necessity of String Theory

If the Big Bang was the most significant discovery about the universe in the twentieth century, then quantum mechanics and general relativity were the greatest physics tools developed to help us understand that discovery. Yet, at the beginning of the twenty-first century, the story took another strange turn! For the past fifty years, scientists have been working hard to understand this Big Bang: to understand the properties of this explosion in its first fraction of a second – when time and space came into being and all the physics processes were set into motion – and to understand the amazing behavior of the universe 14 billion years later, including (perhaps most remarkable of all) how this earth came to be. Despite many breakthroughs in understanding, scientists have also learned about the limitations of their tools. Here is a comment from one of the leaders of the new physics research of the 21st century, Brian Greene of Columbia University, from his famous book, *The Elegant Universe:*

> "For more than half a century, physicists have been quietly aware of a dark cloud looming on a distant horizon. The problem is this: there are two foundational pillars upon which modern physics rests. One is Einstein's general relativity ... the other is quantum mechanics ... As they are currently formulated, general relativity and quantum mechanics cannot both be right."[8]

General relativity and quantum mechanics are theoretical tools that have been confidently applied for decades. But as physicists have tried to apply quantum mechanics and general relativity to understanding the early moments of the Big Bang, when the universe was very small and very dense, it has become apparent that the two theories give different answers, surprisingly when attempting to describe the force that is the most familiar to us: gravity. So there's something wrong. The great pioneer of quantum mechanics, Neils Bohr, once said that "all great theories begin as heresy and end as mythology." By the mid-twentieth century, most scientists had come to accept the universal validity (mythology) of quantum mechanics and general relativity (both born in controversy, i.e., scientific heresy, fifty years earlier). And so by the end of the 20th century -- even though we had all this confidence at the beginning of the 20th century, that we had it all figured out -- we had learned that there is still much missing from our grasp of reality. A new fascination with physics was brewing (not unrelated to the new fascination with science and faith), and the future lay wide open, filled with challenge, excitement, and opportunity.

The problems caused when both general relativity and quantum mechanics are applied to the problem of the Big Bang has demanded a new way of understanding matter on atomic scales. Either the old theories must be revised or new theories are required. One new theory that probably offers the best hope of reconciling relativity and quantum mechanics, while perhaps providing a tool for investigating the earliest moments of the Big Bang, is string theory.

String theory replaces the conventional "standard model" of the universe, which describes matter as being composed of point-like elementary particles electrons and quarks. String theory hypothesizes that all of matter – including the basic particles -- is comprised of very tiny one-dimensional filaments of energy, called 'strings.' They are envisioned to have no thickness, only length. There have been no experiments yet performed that can verify whether or not strings actually exist, as a string is expected to be no more than a hundred billion billion times smaller than an atomic nucleus,[9] and there are many unresolved theoretical problems associated with strings. Yet, a growing community of physicists believes that indeed string theory is our best hope of understanding the very fundamentals of our universe. String theory offers the possibility of understanding all the fundamental particles (and their properties) and explaining all the forces of nature. Yet, if string theory is true, our reality is very strange indeed.

One of the amazing consequences of string theory is that our whole concept of dimensions must be overhauled. You and I understand a three-dimensional world, a reality that has depth, width and height. We know that to get to Joe's apartment, we must go straight down Main Street, turn right and go three blocks up Fifth until we come to his address, then we must go up to the third floor, where he lives – we move in three dimensions. In order to know if the new big-screen TV we just purchased at TV-City will fit into the back of our minivan, we must determine its height, depth, and width. And each of us has height, width and depth, and some of us have more of some than the other, or less, as the case may be, but we've all got some of each. These are all aspects of our familiar three-dimensional world. Einstein, as we have seen, showed that there is a fourth dimension: time.

However, string theory predicts that if indeed we are to build a theory that reconciles quantum mechanics and relativity, explains the properties of the elementary particles, and allows us to calculate properties of the universe in the first moments of the Big Bang -- then we're going to have a fabric of dimensions that doesn't look like our familiar, four-dimensional space at all, but rather is likely to have at least ten dimensions! That, says Brian Greene, is "no fine point. It's a problem!"[10]

Figure 3 shows our familiar three-spatial-dimension world side-by-side with one version of what a ten-dimensional world may look like, a so-called Calabi-Yau space, named for its founders. It's okay if you struggle with visualizing such a space – the best scientists do too, and

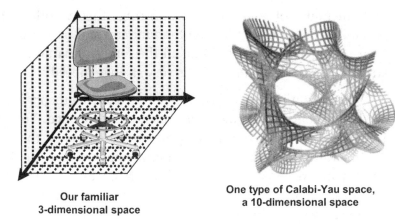

**Our familiar
3-dimensional space**

**One type of Calabi-Yau space,
a 10-dimensional space**

Figure 3 – Familiar things like office chairs seem to have three dimensions. String theory says that office chairs and everything else may exist in a ten or eleven dimensional space, like a Calabi-Yau space.

pictures like this are the best we can do to visualize such a space on a two-dimensional piece of paper. (in fact, the latest version of string theory, called M Theory, asserts that there must be eleven dimensions!) The idea of ten or eleven dimensions boggles our minds, but a good question is why would we ever expect that there would be only three dimensions to begin with? Why not only one or two dimensions? Why not ten or eleven? Okay, it violates our intuition, yes, but most of the physics discoveries of the past century do too.

As the spinning of our heads slows down a bit, we may ask: Wait a minute, if there are more than three spatial dimensions, how come we can't see them? And even if they're all tied in this kind of gobbledy-gooky mess like a Calabi-Yau space, where are they?

Where are they? String theory expert Brian Greene helps us with the following image.[11] He shows how a garden hose viewed from a distance appears to only be a line (that is, it is one-dimensional, having only length). However, as we move closer to the hose, we see that it is actually cylindrical in shape (two dimensional). From a distance we were unable to detect the second (cylindrical) dimension because it is too small to observe. Another example of a "hidden" dimension would be to examine a freeway interchange from a satellite image; it would appear to be two dimensional. Only as we zoom in on the interchange would we see that it has different layers, that is a third dimension (Figure 4).

From far off, the highway system appears two-dimensional

Closer up it is clearly three-dimensional – there is an additional dimension that only appears up close.

Figure 4 – A highway system may contain a hidden dimension when viewed from a distance.

So, the best answer to where the additional dimensions of string theory lie is that they are too small for us to see, although the theory itself gives no guidance to just what size they may be. If we were able to look closer and closer we may see these other dimensions. However, the suspected sizes of these additional dimensions are far too small for us to be able to detect even with our most sensitive instruments at present. No one can visualize exactly what these extra dimensions look like. Yet, it is the best thinking of physicists today.

With the idea of extra dimensions, it's easy for us to let our imaginations run wild. If there are extra dimensions, might there be shortcuts across the universe? Might these extra dimensions be the realm in which God moves and acts? Some have offered such speculations, but this is very dangerous ground for a believer in God to find herself upon, for two reasons.

Some religious commentators have suggested that additional 'hidden' dimensions may be the realm in which God can perform miracles.[12] While I can't say this isn't true, such a suggestion could be the same kind of mistake the church made with Galileo and may have made in pointing to the Big Bang as proof of creation. This is attempting to explain the mysterious ways of God through contemporary scientific theories yet to be proved. Remember the caution of Thomas Aquinas: "Bad explanations for God's existence do more harm than good because they give unbelievers an occasion to laugh." Do not build arguments for things eternal upon a theory that may be refuted in the future. The second danger of explaining God's actions through string theory or any other scientific principle is that it limits God to working through known physical law. It puts God in a box, as we discussed in Chapter 1.

If there are ten or eleven dimensions, you might well ask, "Why do we live in only three dimensions?" Any answer to this question is speculative, but Stephen Hawking has come up with an answer that is at least humorous, if not compelling.[13] He shows us a drawing of a "two-dimensional dog," complete with digestive system, including a mouth for ingesting food and a path for discharging waste. Try drawing your own sketch of such a pooch. This poor pup has a big problem! In order for her to have a digestive system (which is not optional equipment for most animals), the two-dimensional dog exists in two pieces. She will fall apart unless she is designed to be three-dimensional. Hawking suggests that three-dimensional creatures may be a consequence of the anthropic principal - the way it was designed into the fabric of our existence we had to have three dimensions. If there were going to be creatures like us who can live, and have digestive tracts and eat pizza and drink root beer, then we must have at least three dimensions.

Grasping the Mind of God

Modern science has revealed many strange new things about reality. The world of quantum mechanics and string theory is a fascinating world, and it's going to be exciting to see how our physics understanding of it develops in the years ahead. But I think the most amazing thing about the universe is this. The God who created the universe and the laws of physics - - all this amazing stuff that just blows our minds and even baffled Einstein and Richard Feynman – has as his top priority a relationship with us. He created us for his own pleasure and out of his own love. And I think that grasping the love that God has for us is sometimes more difficult than grasping all the intricacies of string theory.

At the end of *A Brief History of Time*, Stephen Hawking writes in anticipation of a complete physics theory of the universe: "Then we shall all, philosophers, scientists, and just ordinary people, be able to take part in the discussion of the question of why it is that we and the universe exist. If we find the answer to that, it would be the ultimate triumph of human reason – for then we would know the mind of God."[14]

But according to our faith, we can already know the mind of God, and it doesn't involve understanding the origin of the universe. It has to do with much more than that. Listen to Philippians 2:5-8:

> Let the *same mind be in you that was in Christ Jesus*, who, though he was in the form of God, did not regard equality with God as something to be exploited, but emptied himself, taking the form of a slave, being born in human likeness. And being found in human form, he humbled himself and

became obedient to the point of death— even death on a cross. (*italics added*)

Having the mind of God is all about love. Love of God and love of our neighbors. This passage tells us that having the mind of God is about living a life of humble service, not seeking power or advantage over others, and striving in all things to be faithful to God.

The Universe and Blueberry Muffins

There is a tendency in our culture to think that scientific discovery of a new physical process or theory (be it natural selection, M theory, or quantum mechanics) somehow transfers that process from the realm of God's doing into the realm of our doing. That is, if we can come up with a theory or speculation, say, about how the Big Bang unfolded over the past 14 billion years, we can now claim to understand the development of the universe without invoking the God of the Bible. This just doesn't make sense.

Let me illustrate. When I was a child, my mother made the best blueberry muffins. They were mouth-wateringly good. When she made these muffins, the house would always be filled with the aroma of the baking muffins, and my anticipation was great for the moment when I would bite into one of those piping-hot wonders. I didn't know how my mother made the muffins – I just assumed she somehow magically produced them – but I always saw those muffins as a special gift to me. They were evidence of her love for me, evidence, in fact, that I had a caring and providing mother.

One day, while reluctantly helping with the dishes, I came across her blueberry muffin recipe. It was right there, printed on a sheet of paper, copied from a cook book. A cookbook that millions of others had no doubt used. I had now discovered the secret of my mom's blueberry muffins. It was no longer a mystery. If I were interested, I could study that recipe and learn exactly how she did it, and even be able to explain it to others. Did my discovery of my mother's blueberry muffin recipe destroy my confidence in her love for me? Did it damage my faith that she would always be there to provide for me? Did it – to really stretch the point – cause me to think that my mother did not, in fact, exist? Of course not!

When we make discoveries about science, we celebrate. Psalm 111:2 says, "Great are the works of the LORD, studied by all who delight in them." Just because we may arrive at new understandings about biology or physics does not now mean that we somehow own the processes, that we can now explain reality and leave God out. No more than I could explain the blueberry muffins of my childhood, without factoring in the reality of my mother and her love for me.

How do we grasp those truly important things in our life? How does a baby learn about the love of its mother? Does the baby do a credit check on its mother? Does the baby check her credentials and say, "Mom, before I invest in loving you, before I trust you, I need to see your resume. Could you prepare that for me?" Does the baby say, "I need to have three references tell me about you?" No, the baby comes to know the mother's love through experience, through touch, through being nurtured, through the affection, through the loving words, through just being there in the presence of mom.

In the first chapter of John's gospel there's a story about Philip finding Nathanael,[15] and saying to him, "We have found him about whom Moses in the law and also the prophets wrote, Jesus, the son of Joseph from Nazareth." This is big news. But Nathanael – with a healthy analytical, questioning, and skeptical mind – does not leap for joy and say, "Yay, let's go! I've been waiting all my life for this!" His response is, "Can anything good come out of Nazareth?" What's amazing is Philip's response to Nathaniel. Philip doesn't launch into a scholarly seminar: "Well, let's look at the history of Nazareth and see if any notable people ever came out of there." That would be one way he could have dealt with Nathaniel's question. Instead, he says simply, "Come and see". Come and see. That's what the baby does. The baby comes and sees the mom and grows into that relationship. It doesn't come to its mom through eliminating all the logical barriers before the relationship begins. As it was with the great theologian Anselm, it is not understanding seeking faith, but faith seeking understanding.

And that's the way it was with my friend Dale. Dale is a very bright electrical engineer, and for his whole life he had been an agnostic. Dale has a wife who is a devout believer, and I later learned that for 17 years his wife had been praying for Dale every day that he would come to know the Lord. And Dale knew that she was praying for him, and he wanted to believe but he just couldn't overcome his intellectual objections. He wanted to make his wife happy, he wanted her prayers to be answered, so he would try to believe, but he just couldn't. He'd say he just couldn't grasp it. It was about at this time that I met Dale in our church. Dale had come to our church a few times before just to please his wife, but this day he came because his wife had heard that I was giving an adult forum talk about science, and so she brought Dale. She was desperately trying anything to expose him to the gospel.

After my talk I sat down and spoke with Dale. He told me, "I've tried everything, but I just can't seem to believe in this God." He said, "I've tried to read the Bible." Now Dale's a perfectly good engineer. You remember the comical definition of an engineer as a guy who has his head in an oven and his feet in a freezer and says, "On the average I'm very comfortable."

Dale told me, "I couldn't go through the whole Bible - it's 2,000 pages long. So I read the first book, Genesis, and the last book, Revelation. I figured that would help me understand everything in between, right?" Perfectly good engineering reasoning. He then added, "I just couldn't get it. Not by a long shot could I get it."

As I sat listening to Dale, I thought, "What do I say to him?" But then, after a few moments of silence, Dale said, "But you know, something is very weird. The last couple of times I came to church - I only came because of my wife - I was just sitting there in the worship service, and all of a sudden I just started crying. I just start crying right in the middle of the service."

He was sure I wouldn't understand. But of course I understood. What was happening was that Dale's relationship with God was building. Dale didn't understand, but like Nathaniel he had come and seen. Dale was bursting into tears because all of his defenses and all of the garbage of his life were being swept away by the love of God.

It was only three weeks later that I had the privilege of standing next to Dale, who, at the age of 37 years old, was baptized. I got to stand there as the water was poured over his head, and as his life was changed. Dale still doesn't understand it all, but who does? We don't understand it all, but the relationship is the whole thing. And Dale has that. And he's living a new life, a joy-filled life.

10. Grasping the Truth

Are the Ways of Knowing in Conflict?

As we survey the world of modern physics, and ponder its connection – if any – to religious faith and our understanding of God, we are led – time and time again – to an intersection that involves many aspects: objective knowledge versus faith, data versus relationship, analysis versus romance. Certainly, almost everyone agrees that the way we navigate through our lives involves all these approaches to understanding truth. Whether the issue is should I ask Mary to marry me, should I mow the lawn today or can it wait another week, how do I respond to a beautiful sunset or a Beethoven piano sonata, or how do I design an experiment to test string theory, both our rational and emotional faculties are drawn upon in varying proportions depending on the question.

Richard Feynman acknowledged that scientific analysis is a powerful tool, but limited to those things which can be subjected to observation:

> "If a thing is not scientific, if it cannot be subjected to the test of observation; this does not mean that it is dead, or wrong, or stupid. We are not trying to argue that science is somehow good and other things are somehow not good. Scientists take all those things that *can* be analyzed by observation, and thus the things called science are found out. But there are some things left out, for which the method does not work. This does not mean that those things are unimportant. They are, in fact, in many ways the most important."[1]

Physicist Paul Davies writes,

> "Perhaps there is a route to knowledge (such as through mysticism or revelation) that bypasses or transcends human reason. As a scientist I would rather try to take human

reasoning as far as it will go. In exploring the frontiers of reason and rationality we will certainly encounter mystery and uncertainty, and in all probability at some stage reasoning will fail us and have to be replaced either by irrational belief or frank agnosticism."[2]

According to Davies and many physicists, you go as far as you can with reason or analysis, then if an answer is still elusive, you either resort to irrational belief or choose not to think about it. Are those really the only options? Certainly, the leading edge of 21st century physics challenges our ability to learn all we want to know through scientific reasoning. Alan Guth, the MIT theoretical physicist who has been responsible for shaping much of modern understanding about the universe and the Big Bang in particular, says,

"There are certain things that we don't understand. We do not understand the foundation of the laws of physics, where they come from, why these are the laws of physics. Whether that should be regarded as deeply mysterious or just a scientific problem for the next century is hard to say."[3]

Yet, when asked if he personally believes in God, Guth responds "I pretty much leave it off the table. When people ask me if I believe in God, I usually ask them to define what they mean by God. The conversation ends there, and that's comfortable."[4]

I can relate to Alan Guth's comments, and for many years my attitude was to keep my scientific thoughts separate from thoughts, if any, I might have about God. Some physicists simply choose not to think about God. This amazes me. Physics is interested in the question: how did the universe come into being? Theology is more interested in the question: Does God exist and what is God like? It is now hard for me to understand how the inquiry of physics does not naturally lead to the inquiry of theology.

But this was not always the case for me, as I like other physicists who do profess a belief in God "manage," as Paul

Davies writes, "to keep these two aspects of their lives separate, as if science rules six days a week, and religion on Sunday."5 I was a Christian and a physicist who kept these two parts of my life separate, not intentionally because of fear or philosophical principle, but because I just didn't connect them in my mind any more than I connected the topic of my child's college education with whether or not the Brewers have a shot at the pennant this year. It was only after my call to ordained ministry that I began to realize that I needed to integrate these two important parts of my life. And when I did, I found, like many scientists, that faith in God and dedication to the principles of scientific research in no way undercut one another. That is, my training as a physicist has not required me to water down or reinterpret my faith in God. Nor has my faith in God required me to deny, distort or refute the solidly-verified findings of modern science. Quite the contrary. I have discovered that faith and science live quite comfortably together, with their unique approaches to revealing the same truth enhancing, not denouncing the other.

Does this mean that all the details of my religious faith can be explained by science? Not at all. Does this mean that I can explain from a biblical perspective all the reality of the universe that science has unmasked in the past century? Nope. You see, for me, science and religious faith give us two different views of the same truth.

Building the House

Let me try to explain using the image of a house under construction. The completed house represents our completed understanding of truth and reality. Science builds upon a foundation of research using the scientific method. Each brick used in the construction is carefully evaluated and understood.

In our scientific pursuit of building the house, which symbolizes our understanding of reality, we are in the very early stages. We are like the entry-level laborer working on the house – we are told which task to perform next, but we have not been given the privilege of seeing the final plans for the house. We do not know what this house will look like when it is completed, and in fact we don't even know what kind of structure it will be. We only know what has already been accomplished. We may see the beginning of the foundation and a few bricks that have been laid in place; these may represent the work of centuries of scientific endeavor, the most recent brick being our grasp of quantum mechanics and general relativity and our experimental observations about the Big Bang. We have laid enough bricks to enable us to develop vaccines for disease and build skyscrapers and Pentium chips. We understand these things well. But we don't know what this structure will be like when it is completed; will it be a mansion, or a store, or a barn? We cannot say, because we only know where the next brick goes (perhaps the first experiments to test string theory). We cannot say, based on this view of the house, anything about morality or the nature of God or his plan, if any, for us.

Faith provides a different view of the house. Through the revelation of Scripture and the ongoing work of the Holy Spirit in the church, we know what the whole house looks like. It is planned by God. We know what its purpose is: to glorify God. We know that there is a place in this house that is designed for us; in fact, we are a part of the house by design. Because we can see the overall shape of the completed house – and we see that it is beautiful and accommodating and planned for us -- we have hope, encouragement and comfort. We find ethical direction and guidance for our lives. We receive everything we need to know about the world to come. Yet, we don't have a good grasp of many other details. We see the completed house, but only as through a fog. Many of the individual bricks may be mysterious to us. Our faith does not give us details about physical reality that would enable us to design a computer, develop a new surgical technique, or measure the size of the universe, nor does it attempt to do so. Scripture tells us that as we peruse this house, even through tightly squinted eyes, we "see through a mirror dimly"[6] We see the whole house but it is a fuzzy outline. Yes, "the mystery of our religion is great."[7] Our fuzzy image is indeed filled with mystery, which means that while we believe the object of our faith is true, we cannot always explain it using scientific language. Yet many believe it is true. As the Book of Common Prayer professes, "We proclaim the mystery of faith: Christ has died, Christ is risen, Christ will come again."[8] That is, God is mysterious, but through faith we know him and can proclaim him confidently to the world.

Please be reminded that faith is built upon a solid foundation of Scripture and the work of the Holy Spirit in the Church, so though our image may be fuzzy, the story is not. The foundation of faith is built on solid ground. The Biblical story tells us clearly that there IS a house. That is, the universe is 1) real, 2) orderly, 3) contingent (that is it could have been made otherwise so we have to study it empirically, rather than deduce it through reason alone), and 4) it is knowable by us because God created us in his image, with a tiny but significant measure of his reason, so that we can – by his grace – explore and learn.[9]

Faith is not about being irrational. Faith is not blind hope. Faith is not some fairy tale we comfort ourselves with against the hardships of life. We do not have faith because of fear. We do not have faith because we abhor reason. Faith is built upon truth, truth that is grasped both with the mind and the heart, with both the thinking and the feeling sides of our being.

What is faith? The writer of the Letter to the Hebrews says that "faith is the assurance of things hoped for, the conviction of things not seen ... by faith we understand that the worlds were prepared by the word of God, so that what is seen was made from things that are not visible."[10] What this whole book has suggested, the writer of Hebrews says in a few words: we grasp the greatest truths through faith. Physics has discovered what God has done, and its accomplishments have been huge, but it is faith that really gives us the big picture, that makes sense of the whole of reality, not by answering when or how, but why. Indeed, faith, as mentioned at the very beginning of this book, enables the confidence that the house of scientific knowledge may proceed, brick by brick.

Eugene Peterson, pastor and writer, says, "You don't look 'faith' up in a dictionary, you look it up in a story."[11] Indeed the whole of Hebrews Chapter 11, sometimes called the Faith Chapter of the Bible, is a series of stories about how people lived in faith. Our faith is not just something we have, it is a way we live. Faith is much more than a rational agreement with the idea of God. Faith is trusting in God, growing in that trust, and making life decisions based on that trust. It is not just something we believe, it is something we do.

It is through faith that we see the picture, albeit it fuzzy, of the whole house. Without faith we must be content with the crisp view of but a few bricks. The house that is built by science is to be studied and analyzed. So is the house built by faith, but its main purpose is to be lived in.

St. Paul reminds us that focus on God demands both the intellect and the deeper knowing of the heart. His guidance: "Set your *hearts* on things above, where Christ is seated at the right hand of God. Set your *minds* on things above, not on earthly things."[12] Faith is stirred from the activity of both intellect and heart.

So while some physicists profess exclusively the use of reason, believers in God are taught to use both the mind and the heart. I have yet to see the ability to solve a differential equation help much in communicating with my children, appreciate the beauty of the sunrise, deal with the death of a friend, appreciate the twinkle in my wife's eye, or grasp what happens in the sacrament of baptism.

Let us be careful, as we intellectually ponder the wonderful developments of modern science, not to diminish the role of the intuitive, the emotional, the feeling. By reason alone, we do not appreciate the lines of a Ferrari or the power of a Mozart symphony. After all, if you only look at it rationally, music is just vibrations on the air.[13]

I would argue that the physicist who claims to use only reason knows how to respond from the heart as well. She knows how to appreciate beauty and joy. And I don't believe this appreciation comes from analysis alone. I don't think I have ever been able to achieve joy by concluding that I should feel it, based upon an equation. However, I have certainly felt joy at times by appreciating the beauty of an equation or the elegance of its solution. Feynman talked about the great "privilege of finding things out" as one of the great motivators for being a physicist. So true. It is more than a privilege, I think, it can be sheer joy. I remember times in the laboratory, after long arduous work in preparing an experiment. It is true that physicists spend most of their work time not reveling in the beauty of nature, or pontificating about new theories and experimental findings. Most of their time is spent in the hard work of getting an experiment to work or a computer program to run without crashing.

There is an old joke that talks about when you walk into a science lab, how you can tell what kind of science is going on there. If it stinks it's chemistry, if it moves it's biology, and if it doesn't work it's physics. So, I have spent my share of time working patiently (and sometimes not so patiently) in fixing vacuum leaks, debugging faulty electronics, calibrating finicky detectors, and getting computer programs to work. But once in awhile, all the pieces come together and there you are alone in the lab at two in the morning after struggling with contrary experimental equipment for eighteen hours straight. And all of a sudden the data begin to come. You are the person privileged to witness some new little truth of creation being revealed. And you get to be the first person in history to see it! It's two in the morning and you are exhausted, yet you are jumping up and down. You want to call someone and tell them, but everyone is asleep. Breaking the news will have to wait until the morning. Such times, although rare, are part of being a physicist. Finding out about things, as Feynman said. It is pure joy! Oh yes, pure joy. A lot of hard rational, analytical work went into this moment, but the experience of it is emotional and joyful.

The psalmist wrote, "The morning stars sang together and all the angels shouted for joy."[14] John Muir, the famed naturalist, wrote, upon seeing the incredible beauty of the California Sierra Nevada mountains, "The morning stars *still* sing together ..."[15] On those two-AM-breakthrough mornings in the lab, I could sense the morning stars still singing together too. For me such times were not only great insights into physics and great relief to have a challenging problem solved, but also a beautiful new glimpse of God's creation. Remember Romans 1:20 (NLT): "From the time the world was created, people have seen the earth and sky and all that God made. They can clearly see his invisible qualities—his eternal power and divine nature. So they have no excuse whatsoever for not knowing God."

I believe it is easy to understand how many physicists can accommodate both a commitment for rational scientific inquiry and a passion for God. What I cannot understand is how anyone can witness the awesome beauty of creation (Alan

Guth says, "If we were to make up the laws of the universe, that universe would be much more dull than the universe we see around us, so there's certainly something there that we don't understand."[16]) and not be driven to seek to know (not just to identify, but to know) the Creator.

The great genius of the TV show *Star Trek* was not the technological imagination that produced transporters and phasors, but rather the fascinating relationship between Dr. Spock, who possessed superior intellect but no feelings, and Captain Kirk, a great intellect in his own right but also a man of romance and emotion. Ultimately, it was Kirk's ability to balance reason and emotion – but employing both – that saved the day. It is why Kirk was captain and Spock was not.

The Bible commands us to love God with all our heart, mind, soul and strength.[17] Seeking to grasp him with the mind only is only a partial grasping at best. As one commentator once said, "Once you've accepted God intellectually, you've only missed it by about seventeen inches, which is roughly the distance between your brain and your heart."

Reaching for the higher ways, the ways of God, requires the use of the heart, that side of us who is the artist, the poet, the lover. Pablo Picasso said, "Every child is an artist. The problem is to remain an artist once he grows up." Scientific inquiry has an element of art in it, as does theology. Original thinking requires it. But somehow the ability to think originally can get burned out of us. J. Robert Oppenheimer, the famed theoretical physicist, is best known for his leadership of the Manhattan Project, the science project that developed the first atomic bomb. He once said that when he was struggling with an especially challenging physics problem, he would take a walk and ask school kids what they thought about it. Of course they did not have a clue about the physics details, but their insights were original because their ability to think originally had not been taught out of them.

In issues of faith and science alike, we are strengthened by using both the mind and the heart. The application of thoughts and feelings must bear fruit, must lead to a response, and I believe the response must be love. St. Paul cautions us, "If I have all faith and all knowledge, but do not have love, then I am nothing."[18] The scientist experiences awe through her exploration and knowledge of the physical world. I believe awe and knowledge should lead to faith. This is where I part ways with those who want to take reasoning as far as it will go, then go no farther. And faith should lead to love. Too often scientists *and* people of faith alike are guilty of standing on the sidelines big time. The scientist may experience the awe and knowledge of the universe, but remain content not to seek a deeper relationship with the one who may be responsible for that universe. Some believers are content to bask in God's love, but not love their neighbor in return: finding the peace of God's blessing on their lives, but remaining blind to the plight of the needy all around them. Love is the logical outpouring of faith. It should be the logical outpouring of reason as well. Shakespeare leaves no doubt: "To be wise and love exceeds man's might" (from *Troilus and Cressida*).

I remember the last time I saw Evan and how his story reveals the incompleteness of a life lived without faith. I was attending a physics conference on the west coast. Many of us had gathered in the main ballroom of the conference hotel to hear one of the great physicists of our field present the plenary lecture. Evan, now up in years, had been a mentor and example to many of us. He had received much acclaim and respect for his work, and this gentle man was well-liked by all of us. We all knew that this lecture might be one of the last, perhaps even the last, that Evan would give before the physics community. So we wanted to hear his ideas about the latest developments in physics, but even more we wanted to hear the insights and remembrances and reflections of a life. Evan began by telling us a funny story, presumably to get the crowd warmed up. He said, "The secret of happiness is to have money, time and energy. The problem is, when you are young you have time and energy, but no money. In your middle years, you have money and energy, but no time. And when you get old, you may have money and time, but no energy." The audience roared, as much out of respect as anything else. I laughed too, but then I leaned forward and looked closer. Was that a bit of mistiness in Evan's eyes? And then I realized that he had been talking about himself. Now, near the end of his life, Evan was looking back and all he could see was a life that had somehow been robbed of its joy. Evan's joke to loosen up the room had actually been a one-minute autobiography. Here was a very successful man by worldly standards, grasping for meaning in his life. If Evan's look at the past revealed disappointment, I wondered what his look into the future produced.

I thought about Evan's formula for success, Happiness = Money + Time + Energy, and how the events of life seem to keep us from ever attaining complete fulfillment. I realized that what Evan had really needed most was not money, time or energy. What he needed most was God. The One who came to comfort the poor, the One who came to refresh the weary, the One who came to make all things possible for those who believe. The One who makes sense out of a life bereft of adequate supplies of money, time and energy.

So this whole story of science and spirituality comes down to this, as we like Evan grasp for meaning and significance in our lives. It comes down to *knowing about* God (if you want to study the universe, if you want to study about creation, ultimately you're studying about God), as opposed to *knowing* God, having a relationship with him. Picture yourself as a traveler, thirsty and exhausted and near death, wandering across the Sahara Desert, fried and baked in the sun. Our traveler makes it to the top of a sand dune, stumbling, almost out of hope, desperate. That's the very situation we find ourselves in, in a life without God. We may choose to not think about it in our life, but that's exactly where we're headed, even the most worldly-successful among us, like Evan. The money, energy, and time we've sought in our life will run out.

As our lost and thirsty traveler comes to the top of the huge sand dune and looks down on the other side, lo and behold there is a pool of water down there! And the water is surrounded by grass and shaded by palm trees, and it's clear and it's beautiful! Now there are two responses that our traveler can have. He can sit there on the top of that sand dune and analyze the situation. Collect data. He can say, "What might be the temperature of that pool? How do I know that the alkalinity in that pool might not be harmful to my health? And how did that pool get there in the first place? Maybe it's just a mirage. It's probably not real." He could ask all kinds of things. He could sit there in the sun, slowly dying and asking these questions. That's what *knowing about* God is like.

Or, he can race down that dune, and plunge into the cool, life-giving water, splashing and rejoicing, bathing and being refreshed and, in fact, having his life saved. That's the difference between *knowing about* God and *knowing* God. And what I want to suggest for everyone of us is that -- while it's good and exciting and beneficial to know about God and to study his creation -- what we need desperately is to know God and to know that life-giving relationship he offers, and to be bathing in the living water of life.

A Short Reading List for Going Deeper

On modern scientific discoveries

Paul Davies, *About Time* (Touchstone, 1995)

Brian Greene, *The Elegant Universe* (Vintage Books, 1999)

Brian Greene, *The Fabric of the Cosmos* (Alfred A. Knopf, 2004)

On science and faith

Ian G. Barbour, *Religion in an Age of Science* (Harper and Row, 1990)

Francis S. Collins, *The Language of God* (The Free Press, 2007).

Alister E. McGrath, *Science and Religion: A New Introduction* (Wiley-Blackwell, 2009).

A. R. Peacocke, *Theology for a Scientific Age* (SCM Press, 1993)

John Polkinghorne, *The Faith of a Physicist* (Princeton University Press, 1994)

On the basics of faith (from my Christian perspective)

C. S. Lewis, *Mere Christianity* (Touchstone, 1943)

John R. W. Stott, *Basic Christianity* (Inter-Varsity Press, 1958)

Study Guide
For personal reflection and small group discussion.

Knowledge and Faith (Chapter 1, pages 5-14)

1. On p. 7 the question is raised, "Perhaps there is one set of truths that apply to science and another set that apply to the spiritual life?" Why might this be an important question and why might a person answer either YES or NO? How do you answer? Why?

2. One theologian has said, "I believe in miracles. I just don't believe that a miracle is an event that will violate the laws of physics." How would you respond to this statement? If this statement is true, how might one explain the resurrection of Christ?

3. Beginning on p. 12, the idea of mystery is discussed. What is the difference between a mystery (which is true) and a superstition (which is not)? How can you tell which is which? Why might many of the proclamations of religion remain a mystery?

4. Einstein said, "The most beautiful emotion we can experience is the mysterious." Why might this be true? What are some examples from your life of such 'beautiful emotions'?

5. How do you respond to the suggestion (p. 10) that there may be a limit to human knowledge? Do you agree or disagree with this idea? What difference does it make?

How Do I Know What's True? (Chapter 2, Pages 15-28)

1.   What are the three objective ways of knowing truth?

2.   Under what circumstances might the scientific method be unreliable? Can you think of an example?

3.   How do you know if a witness is credible?

4.   Several letters from Scripture are cited as reports from witnesses (pp. 25-26). How do you conclude that these witnesses are either trustworthy or untrustworthy?

5.   What kinds of knowledge might not be obtainable through the three objective methods? Why might they not work in these situations?

Another Way of Knowing: Knowing Through Relationship (Chapter 3, Pages 29-37)

1.   How is 'knowing through relationship' different from the three objective ways of knowing discussed in the last chapter?

2.   Knowledge through relationship may often be hard to express or describe (p. 30). Why?

3.   The importance of mentors in learning is discussed on p. 33. When has a mentor been important in your life?

4.   Frederick Buechner says that while we want proof of God's existence, there is something we want even more. What is it? (See bottom of p. 35). How do you respond to his assertion?

5.   How do you respond to the idea that we should use all the ways of knowing? Is this idea more applicable to science or spirituality, or equally important to both?

How a Scientist Thinks About God (Chapter 4, Pages 38-46)

1. Are there findings in modern science that challenge your faith in a divine creator? Are there assertions from your faith tradition that make it difficult for you to accept certain claims of modern science? Can you give some examples?

2. Does an apparent conflict between science and religion mean that either the science is wrong or that the religious claim is wrong? If not, how do you explain such apparent contradictions? (We'll be returning to this topic again in future chapters).

3. According to p. 43, why do scientists have differing views on whether God exists?

4. Read physicist John Polkinghorne's statement (bottom of p. 42) about why he believes in God. Are these credible foundations upon which to build faith? Why or why not?

5. What is the basis upon which you believe that God exists or doesn't exist or you remain uncertain?

Let's be Realistic (Chapter 5, Pages 47-59)

1. What does it mean to be a realistic person? Do you consider yourself a realistic person? Why or why not?

2. The term 'naïve reality' (p. 47) describes how our human perception of reality often falls short of true reality. Why is this an important concept in our discussions about science and spirituality?

3. A scale model of the solar system is described (p. 50) in which the solar system may be accurately envisioned as only a tennis ball (the sun) and a few grains of sand (the planets) scattered over a square mile. And the next nearest large object outside this solar system would be another tennis ball (the star Alpha Centauri) over 2,000 miles away. How do you react to this image?

4. How do you respond to the reality of how large and small, fast and slow, objects and phenomena are, compared with what we can detect with our senses? What does this tell us about drawing conclusions about science, spirituality and their relationship?

5. Read aloud the quote from Isaac Newton on p. 56. What does he mean?

Just a Matter of Time (Chapter 6, Pages 60-73)

1. A child asks you, "What is time?" What would you say?

2. What does the story of Einstein tell you about your own life?

3. How does the theory of relativity violate your intuition about time?

4. "When we react in fear to modern scientific findings, we are not demonstrating faith in God, but rather, I suspect, faith in our naïve reality." (p. 70) How is this true? Please consult the passage from Isaiah, immediately above this comment.

5. This chapter closes with the story of Harold (p. 72). Why do you suppose he continued to be interested in learning about God after so many years? What do you suspect held him back from developing faith? What would you have said to Harold?

Just a Matter of Time, Part 2 (Chapter 7, Pages 74-84)

1. Which is more difficult to comprehend: that the universe is eternal or that the universe (and time) had a beginning? Why?

2. Why does C. S Lewis caution (p. 76) against statements beginning with the words, "Science has now proved ..."?

3. Arno Penzias, who won the Nobel Prize for confirming the Big Bang, said in an interview with the New York Times (p. 76): "The best data we have (concerning the Big Bang) are exactly what I would have predicted, had I nothing to go on but the five books of Moses, the Psalms, and the Bible as a whole." What might you expect about the universe based on your understanding of the Bible?

4. How do you react to the idea (p. 77) that creation is an ongoing process in the universe, and not just its initiation?

5. Is the idea of eternal life an important part of your understanding about God? Why or why not?

What I Did for Love (Chapter 8: Pages 85-110)

1. Why might you conclude that the earth is the center of the universe? Think in terms of your observations and religious ideas.

2. What is the guidance given by St. Augustine (p. 91) that was not heeded by the Church in its interaction with Galileo? How might such guidance be important to us today?

3. "The error of the Church's position on the motion of the earth was in fearing that the concept of an earth that is not the center of everything would diminish the importance of humankind." (p. 93) Why was this fear an error?

4. Summarize in your own words the ideas of the anthropic principle (pages 94-99).

5. Stephen Hawking, in reference to the anthropic principle and the vast complexity of the universe, is quoted on Page 105: "The strong anthropic principle would claim that this whole vast construction exists simply for our sake. This is hard to believe." How would a believer in God respond to this statement? How do you respond?

Small Talk: the Weird World of Quantum Mechanics and Strings (Chapter 9: Pages 111-129)

1. "Doesn't the probabilistic nature of quantum mechanics mean that the outcomes of all atomic scale events are uncertain and therefore the outcome of large scale events must be similarly uncertain and therefore the destiny of the universe is uncertain? Where is there any place for a creative God in a universe like that?" (p. 116) How does the author respond to this question? What issues and concerns does this question raise for you?

2. How do you react to the idea that our physical reality may be comprised of as many as eleven dimensions (p. 121)?

3. If it is likely that strings may never be detected experimentally (because they are so small), should we believe in their existence? Why or why not? You might refer back to Professor Gates' comments on p. 33. What bearing does your answer have on whether one can believe in God?

4. It has been suggested that God may act through the extra dimensions of space predicted by string theory. Why is this a dangerous suggestion (bottom p. 124)?

5. What does Stephen Hawking mean (p. 125) when he talks about having "the mind of God"? What does the Bible (Philippians 2:5-8) say having the mind of God is about (bottom, p. 125)?

Grasping the Truth (Chapter 10, Pages 130-141)

1. The first section of this chapter asks, "Are the ways of knowing in conflict?" How would you summarize the answer?

2. In the image of building the house (p. 132), two ways of seeing the house are described. Which view is most comfortable or appealing to you? Are both views needed?

3. This chapter argues that God must be grasped with both the mind and the heart. Do you agree? Why or why not? What might be the consequences of approaching a topic like faith with either the mind or the heart, but not both?

4. On p. 138 it is argued that the fruit of both knowledge and faith must be love. How do you respond to this? What are some examples of how gaining more knowledge should lead to acts of love? How gaining more faith should lead to acts of love?

5. What is the difference between knowing about God and knowing God?

Acknowledgements

I wish to thank my many friends and colleagues in physics research at the University of California, Riverside; the Argonne National Laboratory; Lawrence Livermore National Laboratory; and Los Alamos National Laboratory. These people make their livings engaging hard questions, and I have grown from their influence, from their thoughtful discussions, insights and encouragement.

I am grateful for many discussions, intelligent questioning, and the active faith and love of members of the parish churches of Trinity on-the-Hill, Los Alamos, New Mexico; St. Mark's on-the-Mesa, Albuquerque, New Mexico; St. Francis on-the-Hill, El Paso, Texas; and Church of the Intercession, Stevens Point, Wisconsin.

I have also benefited greatly from comments from the Rev. Dr. Les Fairfield and the Rev. Dr. Paul F. M. Zahl on an early draft of this book. Les Fairfield provided especially important insights on the subjective ways of knowing. I am grateful to the parishes of St. Joseph's Episcopal Church, Buena Park, California, and St. Stephen's Episcopal Church, Whittier, California (The Rev. M. P. Trainor, Vicar) for using an early draft of this book for small group study and providing useful guidance for its improvement—the insights and comments from Bob Henkle and Christopher Potter are especially appreciated. I also thank William Dorsey for help in the editing of an early draft.

I thank Lea Magruder for typing the initial draft of the book.

Finally, I am greatly indebted to my wife Mary for her encouragement, helpful critiquing of this manuscript, love and so much more.

REFERENCES

Chapter One – Knowledge and Faith

1. Richard P. Feynman, *The Meaning of it All: Thoughts of a Citizen-Scientist* (Reading, MA: Perseus Books, 1998), p. 35

2. Stephan Gould, quoted by Jean Pond, *Science and Christianity: Four Views*, Richard Carlson, Ed. (Downer's Grove: InterVarsity Press, 2000), p. 81.

3. The Book of Common Prayer, p. 877.

4. Deuteronomy 29:29

5. St. Thomas Aquinas, *On the Truth of the Catholic Faith: Summa Contra Gentiles*, trans. Anton C. Pegis (New York: Doubleday, 1955) Book I, p. 78.

6. Isaiah 55:9

7. Stephen Hawking, *A Brief History of Time* (New York: Bantam, 1988), p. 175.

8. J. Bardeen, L. N. Cooper, and J. R. Schrieffer, "Theory of Superconductivity", *The Physical Review* **108**, 1175 (1957). I remember when I first read this classic paper in graduate school. As the authors logically and clearly explained one formerly mysterious property of superconductors after the other, I had the feeling that I was being given insight into real truth.

9. 1 Timothy 3:16

10. 1 Corinthians 13:12

11. Albert Einstein, "What I Believe", quoted by Walter Isaacson, *Einstein, His Life and Universe* (New York: Simon and Schuster, 2007), p. 387.

12. Albert Einstein, quoted by Walter Isaacson, *Einstein, His Life and Universe* (New York: Simon and Schuster, 2007), p. 386

Chapter Two – How do I know if it's true?

1. James Reston, Jr., *Galileo, A Life* (New York: HarperCollins, 1994), p. 30

2. 1 Corinthians15:3-6 (New Living Translation)

3. 1 John 1:1-2

4. Acts 4:13

5. Hebrews 12:1-2

6. *The First Detection of The Neutrino by Frederick Reines and Clyde Cowan*, Dennis Silverman, Online from the Physics Department of the University of California, Irvine:
http://www.ps.uci.edu/physics/news/nuexpt.html. This reference also contains references to some of the original papers on neutrino detection.

7. *Celebrating the Neutrino*, Los Alamos Science, Number 25, 1997.

8. Romans 10:13-14

Chapter Three –Another Way of Knowing

1. Bishop Edward Little, Diocesan Clergy Retreat, Diocese of Fond du Lac, February, 2006.

2. Esther Lightcap Meek, *Longing to Know – The Philosophy of Knowledge for Ordinary People*, (Grand Rapids: Brazos Press, 2003), p. 140

3. Quoted in Karl Stern, *The Flight from Woman* (St. Paul: Paragon House, 1965), p. 43

4. Gary Deddo, "The Priority of personal Knowledge in the Thought of C. S. Lewis", *The Princeton Theological Review*, April/May 1999, p. 29.

5. John 14:8-9

6. Psalm 34:8

7. Matthew 28:20

8. Stern, p. 49.

9. Matthew 22:37

10. Acts 17:11

11. *The Elegant Universe*, a NOVA television program on public television, produced by WGBH/Boston, 2003.

12. Stern, p. 54.

13. Hebrews 11:1

14. Meek, p. 16

15. Paul Davies, *The Mind of God* (New York: Touchstone, 1992), p. 204.

16. Frederick Buechner, *The Magnificent Defeat* (San Francisco: Harper, 1966), p. 44.

17. *Ibid*, p. 47.

18. Hebrews 13:5

Chapter Four – How a Scientist Thinks About God

1. Leslie Fairfield, History of the Church of England, Trinity Episcopal School for Ministry, Ambridge, PA, unpublished].

2. John Gribbin, *The Scientists* (Random House, 2002). p. 181.

3. James Gleick, *Isaac Newton* (Vintage Book, 2003), p. 183.

4. Even today any modern freshman physics book begins with an overview of the physics principles that Newton developed, so-called classical physics. A good example is Raymond Serway and John Jewett, *Principles of Physics, 3rd Edition* (Orlando: Harcourt, 2002).

5. Gleick, p. 186.

6. Justo Gonzalez, *The Story of Christianity, Volume II*, (SanFrancisco: HarperSanFrancisco, 1985), p. 189

7. JRH Moorman, *A History of the Church in England*, (Harrisburg: Morehouse, 1980), p. 256.

8. B. M. G. Reardon, *Religious Thought in the Victorian Age*, Second Edition, (London: Longman, 1995), pp. 211-212

9. Francis S. Collins, *The Language of God*, (The Free Press, 2007) and the ongoing discussions at www.biologos.com. To argue that one must choose between a theory of evolution and the doctrine of a universe created by a God is, in my opinion, simplistic. Evolution does preclude the action of a creator and sustainer, and the biblical story of creation does not preclude a guided process.

10. B. M. G. Reardon, p. 243.

11. Publications such as *Essays and Reviews* (1860) and *Lux Mundi (1899)*, written by church scholars, evidenced a new and almost complete embrace of human reason over revelation as a vehicle for grasping God. Against these trends of the late 19th century stands this comment from John Polkinghorne, more reflective of 21st century appreciation of science and theology: "A very ordinary scientist today possesses ... much greater overall understanding of the physical world than was ever possible for Sir Isaac. The situation in theology is entirely different. The Object of its study is not open to manipulation, nor can he be caught in our rational nets. Every encounter with divine reality has the character of gracious gift and it partakes of the uniqueness inherent in any personal meeting. The theologian of the twentieth century enjoys no presumptive superiority over the theologians of the fourth or sixteenth centuries. Indeed, those earlier centuries may well have had access to spiritual experiences and insights which have been attenuated, or even lost, in our own time." [John Polkinghorne, *Faith of a Physicist* (Princeton: Princeton University Press, 1994), p. 7].

12. Quoted by Natalie Angier in *Confessions of a Lonely Atheist*, New York Times Magazine, January 14, 2001, p. 37

13. John Polkinghorne, *Religion in an Age of Science*, the McNair Lecture, presented at University of North Carolina, Chapel Hill, March 23, 1993.

14. Alister McGrath, *The Dawkins Delusion* (Downers Grove: IVP Books, 2007), p. 44.

15. Henry F. Schaefer, *Science and Christianity: Conflict or Coherence* (Watkinsville: Apollos Trust, 2003), p. 11.

16. "Why God Became Man," trans. Fairweather in *A Scholarly Miscellany: Anselm to Ockham*, pp. 101-102.

17. Romans 1:20 (New Living Translation)

18. John Polkinghorne, *The Faith of a Physicist* (Princeton University Press, 1994), p. 63.

Chapter Five – Let's be Realistic

1. "The National Ignition Facility Comes to Life," Lawrence Livermore National Laboratory, *Science and Technology 2003*, http://www.llnl.gov/str/September03/Moses.html. Also see the updated news on NIF at https://lasers.llnl.gov/.

2. Tom Siegfried, "In Praise of Hard Questions," *Science*, Vol. 309, Issue 5731, p. 76, July 1, 2005.

3. Brian Greene, *The Fabric of the Cosmos* (Alfred A. Knopf, 2004), p. 5.

4. Brian Greene, *The Elegant Universe* (New York: Vintage Books, 1999), p. 207

5. John 1:18

6. 1 Timothy 3:16

7. D. Brewster, *Memoirs of Newton,* Vol. ii. Chap. xxvii. (1855).

Chapter Six – Just a Matter of Time

1. Information on Einstein's youth is taken from Denis Brian, *Einstein, A Life*, New York: John Wiley, 1996, pp. 4-30.

2. Raymond Serway and John Jewett, *Principles of Physics, 3rd Edition* (Orlando: Harcourt, 2002), p. 282*ff*. This treatment is typical of that found in modern introductory texts for physics students.

3. These and other experiments on time dilation are nicely described by Paul Davies, *About Time* (New York:Touchstone, 1995), pp. 55-58.

4. 1 Corinthians 1:19

5. John 20:31

6. Isaiah 45:9-12

7. 1 Corinthians 2:1-4

8. H. Rolston, *Science and Religion*, Temple University Press, 1987, p. 66 (quoted by John Polkinghorne, *The Faith of a Physicist*, Princeton University Press, 1994, p. 28)

9. Will and Ariel Durant, *The Age of Reason Begins* (New York: Simon and Schuster, 1961), p. 607.

Chapter Seven – Just a Matter of Time, Part 2

1. Paul Davies, *The Mind of God* (New York: Touchstone, 1992), pp. 45-50. Davies gives a good survey of belief about and problems with an infinite, eternal universe.

2. Brian Greene, *The Elegant Universe* (New York: Vintage Books, 1999), p. 348 – Contains a good popular discussion of testing the Big Bang.

3. Data from NASA's Wilkinson Microwave Anisotropy Probe have narrowed the age of the universe to 13.7 billion years (NASA news conference, February 11, 2003, reported by CBS News).

4. St. Augustine, *Confessions*, Book 11, Chapter 13, transl. R. S. Pine-Coffin (London: Penguin, 1961), p. 263.

5. Pope Pius XII, "Un Ora," p 31-43 v 44, *Acta Apostolicae Sedis—Commentarium Officiale*, 1952.

6. C. S. Lewis, *God in the Dock*, ed. Walter Cooper (Grand Rapids: Eerdmans, 1970), p.92.

7. Will and Ariel Durant, *The Age of Reason Begins* (New York: Simon and Schuster, 1961), p. 608.

8. Interview with the *New York Times*, March 12, 1978, quoted in Henry F. Schaefer, *Science and Christianity: Conflict or Coherence* (Watkinsville: Apollos Trust, 2003), p. 49.

9. Paul Davies, *The Mind of God* (New York: Touchstone, 1992), p. 177*ff*

10. Gordon Kane, *Supersymmetry: Unveiling the Ultimate Laws of Nature* (Cambridge: Perseus Publishing, 2000), p. 136*ff.*

11. John Polkinghorne, *Science and Theology, An Introduction* (London:SPCK, 1998), p.80.

12. John 20:28-29

13. John 1:1.

14. John 8:53-58

15. Hebrews 13:5

16. C. S. Lewis, *A Severe Mercy,* Letter to Sheldon Vanauken (23 December, 1950), p. 93.

Chapter Eight – What I Did for Love

1. Stephen Hawking, *A Brief History of Time* (New York: Bantam, 1988), p. 171

2. Alister E. McGrath, *Science and Religion: An Introduction* (Blackwell Publishers, 1999), p. 194.

3. Woody Allen, from the movie *Annie Hall,* 1977.

4. Quoted in Patrick Glynn, *God: The Evidence* (Rocklin: Prima Publishing, 1999), p. 36

5. Will and Ariel Durant, *The Age of Reason Begins* (New York: Simon and Schuster, 1961), p. 608

6. Hawking, p. 126

7. Max Tegmark, *Parallel Universes*, Scientific American, May, 2003.

8. John Gribbin, *The Scientists* (Random House, 2002). P. 86.

9. Peter Machamer, *The Cambridge Companion to Galileo* (Cambridge: Cambridge University Press, 1999), p. 224

10. Durant, p. 605

11. Dava Sobel, *Galileo's Daughter* (New York: Penguin, 2000), p. 5

12. Gribbin, p. 95

13. Durant, p. 606

14. St. Augustine, *The Literal Meaning of Genesis*, tr. John Hammond Taylor, in *Ancient Christian Writers: The Works of the Fathers in Translation*, no. 41 (New York: Newman Press, 1982), vol. 1, pp. 42-43.

15. Sobel, p. 274.

16. *Ibid.*, p. 313.

17. John Leslie, *Universes* (London: Routledge, 1989), pp. 1-6, 25-65, contains one of the first summaries published.

18. Hawking, p. 127.

19. Stephen M. Barr, *Modern Physics and Ancient Faith* (Notre Dame: Univ. of Notre Dame Press, 2003), Chapter 15, p. 118*ff*, presents a good review of several of the "anthropic coincidences."

20. Brian Greene, *The Fabric of the Cosmos* (New York: Knopf, 2004), p. 353.

21. Stephen C. Meyer, "Modern Science and the Return of the God Hypothesis," *Science and Christianity: Four Views*, Richard Carlson, editor (Downers Grove: InterVarsity, 2000), p. 147.

22. Leslie, p. 204.

23. Gordon Kane, *Supersymmetry* (Cambridge: Perseus Publishing, 2000), p. 142.

24. Quoted by John Polkinghorne, *The Faith of a Physicist* (Princeton University Press, 1994), p. 55.

25. Hawking, p. 174.

26. John Polkinghorne, *Science and Theology* (London: SPCK, 1998), p. 37.

27. Freeman Dyson, quoted in John D. Barrow and Frank J. Tipler, *The Anthropic Cosmological Principle* (London: Oxford University Press, 1988), p. 318

28. Owen Gingerich, *God's Universe* (Cambridge: Harvard University Press, 2006), p. 12.

29. A good survey of shortcomings in our current theoretical understanding of the universe can be found in Gordon Lane, "The Dawn of Physics Beyond the Standard Model," *Scientific American*, June 2003, p. 69; for more detail see Craig J. Hogan, *The Little Book of the Big Bang: A Cosmic Primer*, Copernicus Books, 1998.

30. John Henry Newman, quoted by E. T. Oakes, Books in Review, *First Things* 109, January, 2001, pp. 48-52

31. 1 Corinthians 2:9

32. Richard Dawkins, *The God Delusion* (New York: Houghton-Mifflin, 2006), p. 5.

33. *Ibid.*, p. 158.

34. *Ibid.*, p. 141.

35. *Ibid.*, p. 140.

36. *Ibid.*, p. 109

37. *Ibid.*, p. 125.

38. *Ibid.*, p. 109.

39. Alister McGrath, *The Dawkins Delusion* (Downers Grove: IVP Books, 2007), p. 28.

40. *Ibid.*, p. 13.

41. *Ibid.*, p. 11.

42. Francis S. Collins, *The Language of God* (New York: Free Press, 2006), p. 164.

43. Ibid., Chapter 10, 197*ff* and the website www.biologos.net.

44. Freeman Dyson, The Templeton Lecture, 2000.

45. Peter Atkins, "There is No God," *The World and I*, May, 2001.

46. Quoted in Ian Barbour, *When Science Meets Religion* (San Francisco: HarperCollins, 2000), p. 155.

47. Collins, p. 223.

48. *Ibid.*, p. 222.

49. John Polkinghorne, *The Faith of a Physicist* (Princeton University Press, 1994), p. 17.

50. Paul Davies, *The Mind of God* (New York: Touchstone, 1992), p. 232.

51. Jeremiah 29:15

52. Romans 12:12

53. 2 Corinthians 4:6

54. Hawking, p. 126.

55. 2 Peter 3:8

56. Archbishop Desmond Tutu, *Spiritual Formation Conference (Sponsored by Trinity Wall Street Church)*, Camp Allen, Texas, March, 2003.

57. 1 Corinthians 13:2

58. Genesis 1:26-31

59. Mark 12:30

60. John 3:16

61. Isaiah 53:4-5

62. 1 John 4:19

63. John 13:34-35

64. Lamentations 3:22-23.

65. 1 John 4:16

66. 1 Corinthians 13:13

67. John 21:15

68. Romans 8:38-39

Chapter Nine – Small Talk: The Weird World of Quantum Mechanics and Strings

1. Quoted in Brian Greene, *The Elegant Universe* (New York: Vintage Books, 1999), p. 86.

2. Brian Greene, *The Fabric of the Cosmos* (New York: Knopf, 2004), p. 11.

3. Psalm 111:1-2.

4. Henry F. Schaefer, *Science and Christianity: Conflict or Coherence* (Watkinsville: Apollos Trust, 2003), p. 115.

5. *Ibid.*, p. 107-120

6. Ian G. Barbour, *When Science Meets Religion* [San Francisco: HarperCollins, 2000], pp. 65-89.

7. John Polkinghorne, *The Faith of a Physicist* (Princeton University Press, 1994), p. 46.

8. *The Elegant Universe*, p. 3

9. *The Fabric of the Cosmos*, p. 345.

10. *Ibid.*, p. 359.

11. *The Elegant Universe.*, p. 186

12. This is discussed in Barbour, p. 46

13. Stephen Hawking, *A Brief History of Time* (New York: Bantam, 1988), p. 164.

14. Ibid., p. 171.

15. John 1:45

Chapter Ten – Grasping the Truth

1. Richard Feynman, *The Meaning of it All: Thoughts of a Citizen-Scientist* (Reading, MA: Persius Books, 1998) p. 16.

2. Paul Davies, *The Mind of God* (New York: Touchstone, 1992), p. 24.

3. From an interview with Alan Guth, *Our Inflationary Universe*, "Research News and Opportunities in Science and Technology", July/August, 2003, p. 5.

4. *Ibid.*, p.5.

5. *The Mind of God*, p. 15.

6. 1 Corinthians 13:12.

7. 1 Timothy 3:16.

8. The Book of Common Prayer, p. 362.

9. I am grateful to Les Fairfield for pointing out these conclusions.

10. Hebrews 11:1-3

11. Eugene H. Peterson, "Follow the Leader," Washington Island Forum, sponsored by Wisconsin Council of Churches, July 11-15, 2005.

12. Colossians 3:1-2, emphasis mine.

13. John Polkinghorne, *Searching for Truth* (New York: Crossroad, 1996), p. 61.

14. Psalm 38:7

15. John Muir, "Explorations in the Great Tuolumne Cañon," *Overland Monthly*, August, 1873; *John of the Mountains*, (1938), page 72.

16. Guth, p. 5

17. Matthew 22:37

18. 1 Corinthians 13:2

About the Author

Jim Trainor is both a physicist and ordained priest. He holds a Ph. D. in physics from the University of California and was active in physics research for over twenty-five years, serving in some of the world's premier scientific laboratories. He is also an ordained Episcopal priest and has served as senior pastor to congregations in New Mexico, Texas, and Wisconsin. He and his wife Mary have three grown children and one brilliant Golden Retriever.

Jim's website: www.JimTrainorAuthor.com

Made in the USA
Monee, IL
22 September 2024

66364663R00098